ASPECTS OF CHESTERFIELD

Aspects of
CHESTERFIELD
Discovering Local History

Edited by
Geoffrey Sadler

Series Editor
Brian Elliott

Wharncliffe Books

First Published in 2002 by
Wharncliffe Books
an imprint of
Pen and Sword Books Limited,
47 Church Street, Barnsley,
South Yorkshire. S70 2AS

For up-to-date information on other titles produced under the
Wharncliffe imprint, please telephone or write to:

> **Wharncliffe Books**
> **FREEPOST**
> **47 Church Street**
> **Barnsley**
> **South Yorkshire S70 2BR**
> **Telephone (24 hours): 01226 - 734555**

ISBN: 1-903425-25-5

A CIP catalogue record of this book is available from the
British Library

Cover illustration: *A view of Chesterfield from the canal by H Ryde (1893).*

Printed in the United Kingdom by
CPI UK

CONTENTS

INTRODUCTION

by

Geoffrey Sadler

Over the years, the town of Chesterfield has been the subject of many different historical studies, but it seems fair to claim that the present publication comes as something of a 'first'. The *Aspects* series has been run for several years with great success by Wharncliffe Books in its native Yorkshire, where it has justly enjoyed a high regard, but this treatment has not previously been afforded to North Derbyshire's largest market town. With the appearance of this volume, aimed both at students of Chesterfield's past and the more general reader of local history, that situation is about to change.

Aspects of Chesterfield approaches its subject from the broadest of angles, and although primarily concerned with the town itself, casts its investigative net rather wider. The splendidly named Charles Dickens draws on his personal experience in presenting his memories of life in Arkwright Town, a former mining village lying three miles east from Chesterfield, as a child in the 1950s, and later as a miner in the colliery, before its demolition and the erection of a new village on the far side of the road. In contrast with this account by a graduate from the 'university of life', Dr David Edwards provides us with a model of scholarly research in his discussion of *Wingerworth: a 'Close' Parish?*, where he utilises not only an excellent academic background but also his thirty-five years' study of Wingerworth village, a close neighbour of Chesterfield on its south-western side. Brampton and Whittington, now Chesterfield districts, were formerly independent parishes in their own right. Trevor Nurse, former college lecturer and long-term Whittington native, gives a fascinating account of one of his village's earliest industries, the Whittington Glasshouse established by the Dixon family in the eighteenth century. His text is further enriched by several of his original line drawings. John Lilley's personal recollections of Brampton, once an industrial powerhouse noted for its potteries and collieries, as well as its entertainments and characters, gain an added authority from the wealth of local knowledge he possesses as a Brampton-born 'native son' and a long-serving Local Studies

Librarian. In similar vein, Sonia Preece offers a time-traveller's perspective on the ancient district of Spital, once part of Hasland parish but now firmly within Chesterfield, from its earliest days as the site of St Leonard's Leper Hospital to the present time.

Further facets of the historic town are explored in the remaining articles. David Howes, who for many years has combined the roles of hairdresser and historian, proves an ideal narrator in *Tricks of the Trade* for his study of three leading Chesterfield entrepreneurs – John Turner, J K Swallow, and John Roberts. His article is a timely reminder of the importance of these and fellow tradesmen to a town whose prosperity has always rested on its success as a centre for commerce. Lynne Patrick, well known in the town as arts and theatre critic of the *Derbyshire Times*, reveals the considerable extent of her knowledge and skills as a journalist and freelance writer in her striking account of Chesterfield's theatrical history, opening up an unexpected window on the town's cultural past. Social history is also examined by David Botham, whose study explores that early example of welfare and educational provision, Chesterfield Ragged School, from its beginnings in the central slums known as the Dog Kennels to its years as a school for the poor, and afterwards as a place of worship. Peter Hawkins' long years of service, together with those of his interviewees, as veteran employees of Markham & Co, ensure a first-hand authenticity in his history of a company which for almost a century stood in the forefront of Chesterfield's manufacturing and engineering industries. Brian Austin, familiar to Cestrefeldians as a keen researcher into the town's characters and customs, takes an oblique look at the nineteenth century tradition of Twelfth Night and Monster Cakes that were a highlight of the Victorian year, a tradition which in slightly altered form endures to this day. Carol Brindle, in *Ghosts of Chesterfield*, forsakes the corporeal world for the domain of the spirits, tracing the invisible footsteps of the town's most famous spectres. As one long familiar with their haunting-places, she is eminently well qualified to recount this most eerie aspect of Chesterfield and its past.

I would like to express my grateful thanks to all my contributors, each of whom matches an impressive knowledge with a genuine enthusiasm and feeling for the subject. Thanks must also go to Chesterfield Local Studies Library and Derbyshire Library Service, to the Pomegranate Theatre, Mrs G M Wilsher, Alan Hill Books, and Kvaerner Markham of Sheffield for their kind permission for the copying of photographs, and to the Ordnance Survey for permission to reproduce sections from Old County Series maps. Every effort has been made to establish copyright for the images shown in the text, and if I have failed to acknowledge any original copyright holder here, I hope they will accept my sincere apologies, and the assurance that I did my very best to find them. Thanks also to the numerous kind providers of information, to Brian Davis for the copying of archive photographs, and to Dennis Middleton for the original photographs supplied in the text. Finally, my sincere thanks to Brian Elliott and his colleagues at Wharncliffe Books for thinking of me in connection with this work, and for their help and advice in bringing it about.

1. THOSE DANCE BAND DAYS
THE RISE AND FALL OF CHESTERFIELD'S RENDEZVOUS DANCE HALL

by Geoffrey Sadler

LESS THAN SEVENTY YEARS AGO, the area around Sheffield Road echoed to the sound of music as dance-crazy couples flocked to the entertainment nightspot of their choice. There, at an outwardly unprepossessing building, as many as 400 would crowd the floor and dance the night away to the smooth playing of some of the leading dance bands in the country. Every night they travelled here from all over the East Midlands, for this was the famous 'Rendezvous' dance hall, one of the best entertainment venues around.

Anyone visiting the place now would find it hard to believe that such a thing ever happened. The building has long since been levelled to the ground after being gutted by fire in the early 1990s, and no trace of it remains. Nevertheless, its existence was real enough, as were the varied uses to which it was put in the decades spanning 1920-50. In order to tell the story fully, we had better start at the beginning.

The Burkitt Malthouse
It began life in the 1850s, a fact confirmed by the *Map of the Borough of Chesterfield* drawn by Thomas Ward and Richard Hugh Burman.[1] This 1858 map shows the building on its site west of Sheffield Road below Trinity Walk and sharing its grounds with St Helen's House, later part of St Helena School; later, the 1878 Ordnance Survey 1:500 scale enlargement (Figure 1) identifies it as a malthouse.[2] It was owned by the Burkitt family, prosperous corn and seed merchants involved in overseas trade with Europe and the United States. William Burkitt supervised all the maltings in the Chesterfield area from his residence at St Helen's House, and on his death in 1898 the operation passed to his son, another William. The Sheffield Road malthouse remained in the family until he too died in 1920. Soon afterwards, under new ownership, it took on a more glamorous role, in the first of two separate phases as a dance hall.

Evening Dress Essential: the 'Rendezvous Palais de Danse' 1925-30
In the early 1920s the Sheffield Road building was acquired by Colin

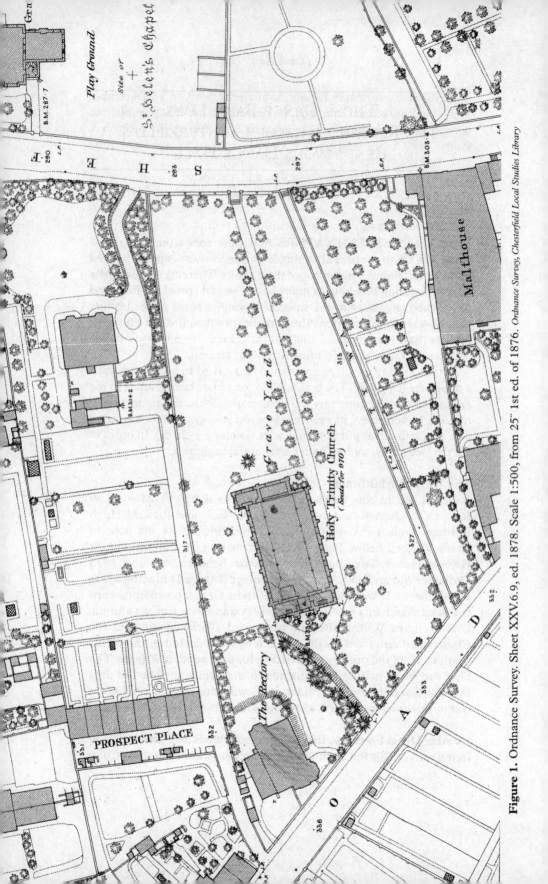

Figure 1. Ordnance Survey. Sheet XXV.6.9, ed. of 1878. Scale 1:500, from 25" 1st ed. of 1876. *Ordnance Survey, Chesterfield Local Studies Library*

Richardson, a gentleman farmer from Derby, who on 16 December 1924 secured official approval for an ambitious building plan to convert the old malthouse to a dance hall.[3] Architects Wilcockson & Cutts, and Chesterfield builder Thomas Tomlinson, were given the task, and the conversion was completed early in 1925.

The transformation was startling and deceptive. The outside of the building stayed virtually unaltered from its days as a malthouse, but once inside the place was a revelation, with large dance floor, staircase leading to a vestibule with cloak rooms, supper room and buffet facilities. Balconies overhung the polished maplewood dance floor, and the blue-painted décor with gold framed mirrors on the walls was topped by open Tudor-style rafters and massive oak beams. The lighting effects introduced by Mr Richardson sound remarkably modern for the mid-1920s. In his report shortly before the official opening, the *Derbyshire Times* correspondent informed readers that:

> *In addition to the large glass chandeliers there will be a number of strip lights running along the beams and these can be changed to red, yellow, blue or amber. In order to facilitate these changes the switch board attendant will be connected by telephone with the ballroom and receive his instructions from the manager. In addition there will be limelight effects with the latest rainbow attachment, a very effective system of varying the light.*[4]

He also praised the elaborate system of ventilation housed in the upper storey of the building, which ensured a complete change of air three times an hour.

The hall opened to dancers on 1 April 1925 as the 'Rendezvous Palais-de-Danse', the event being attended by 300 invited guests, including some from Derby and Sheffield. All were suitably dazzled by the luxurious appearance of the hall with its chandeliers, mirrors and floral decorations, and by the ingenious lighting effects. The polished maple dance floor (Figure 2), laid by Messrs Hollis of Hull, came in for particular praise, being hailed as 'by far the best floor in the county.'[5] John and Julia Harvey (or Hervey), leading ballroom dancers from London, gave a demonstration of exhibition dancing, and music was provided by two bands playing alternate sets throughout the evening. The opening was a great success, as was the first public dance the following evening, which once again drew a large attendance.

Following this successful launch, the 'Rendezvous' management established a regular pattern of dances, each night given over to a

Figure 2. Inside the 'Rendezvous' in 1928, showing the polished maplewood dance floor. *Photograph donated by Mr Arthur Hawes to Chesterfield Local Studies Library*

particular event or speciality. A *Derbyshire Times* advertisement for 18 April 1925 (Figure 3) details Carnival Night, Special Night (Evening Dress Essential), Novelty Dance and a Police Benefit Ball. It also includes two afternoon Tea Dances, a regular feature in the years to come. The musicians, 'the Celebrated Cabaret Players', were probably a Leicester-based band. The tone for the 'Rendezvous' was now set. The *de luxe* nature of the ballroom, its professional staff and musicians, coupled with Mr Richardson's insistence on the highest standards and formality of dress, were obviously aimed at the more affluent patrons in the town. This was a costly venture on his part, and one by no means certain of success. Nevertheless, the dance hall continued its high-class operation for the next five years, attracting the 'better class' of customer. Closed for improvements in June 1925, it re-opened in September with its dance floor re-polished, and armed with a new dancing programme. The manager, John Harvey, claimed to have gone to Paris to 'obtain the very latest dances', and had hired several leading professionals, among them 'a well known operatic and step dancer'.[6] Staff undertook to give lessons to patrons at the hall or in private houses, children's dances and dance competitions were added to the repertoire, and on the Special Night event of 8 September the 'new Charleston dance' was demonstrated. Mr Richardson proudly announced that: 'We teach the West End of London style of dancing and have the finest dance band of four in the Midlands.'[7] Among those who remember the 'Rendezvous' of 1925-30 is Mrs Marjorie Rawicz, wife of author Slavomir Rawicz (of *The Long Walk* fame) and herself later to be Chesterfield's first Children's Librarian. She recalls taking part in the children's dances with her sister at the hall:

We gave several displays, the principal one I recollect when I danced a Jockey Dance, and my sister dressed as a fairy emerged out of a huge Christmas pudding. The music was played on a gramophone as I distinctly remember the Jockey tune as being Sousa's Blaze Away.[8]

Figure 3. Progamme of dancing at the 'Rendezvous', as advertised in the *Derbyshire Times* of 18 April 1925. *Derbyshire Times*

THE "RENDEZVOUS" DANCE HALL.
SHEFFIELD ROAD, CHESTERFIELD.

MONDAY, APRIL 20th —
    GRAND CARNIVAL NIGHT DANCING ... ... 7 to 11 - 1/-

TUESDAY, APRIL 21st —
    SPECIAL NIGHT (Evening Dress Essential)... ... ... 7 to 11 - 5/-

WEDNESDAY, APRIL 22nd -
    CINDERELLA DANCE (Heap of Novelties) ... ... 7 to 11 - 2/-
    TEA DANCE ... ... 3 to 5.30 - 1/6

THURSDAY, APRIL 23rd -
    A GRAND BALL (Chesterfield Borough Police in
    aid of the Widows and Orphans Fund)
      Dancing 8 p.m to 2 a.m. ... ...   Admission 2/6

FRIDAY, APRIL 24TH -
    REQUEST NIGHT 1/6

SATURDAY, APRIL 25th -
    CARNIVAL NIGHT ... ... 7 to 11 - 2/6
    TEA DANCE ... ... 3 to 5.30 - 1/6

THE CELEBRATED CABARET PLAYERS ALWAYS IN ATTENDANCE.

One of the professional dancers hired by John Harvey was Arthur Hawes, who was employed at the 'Rendezvous' from late 1925 until 1928, as Chief of Staff and Senior Dance Instructor.

We had what was known as a pen, where myself, another fellow and two females were able to dance with the patrons who had bought a 6d ticket for one dance with us.[9]

His memories are confirmed by Mr and Mrs Albert Daykin, who attended during this period. Mrs Daykin, then Miss Edith Wright, was also a dancer at the 'Rendezvous', and identifies the others as Leslie Barton, Elsie Bradford and 'A N Other' (presumably Mr Hawes.)[10] Mr Daykin, a dance band saxophonist , was also a skilful dancer, and he and his wife won the Charleston competition at the 'Rendezvous' in 1926. There was no let-up to the dancing throughout that year, (Figure 4) with a full programme of Tea Dances and Foxtrot and Tango competitions. In February Mr Richardson proudly announced the appearance of 'Monsieur Pierre, the Great Exponent of Modern Ballroom Dancing'. This eminent gentleman was to provide 'demonstrations of the Latest Tango as Danced in Paris (*shades of Marlon Brando!*), the Paso Doble, the New One-Step, Waltz and Foxtrot', for the fairly exclusive price of 3s (15p).[11] On 1 April the hall celebrated its first year with a Birthday Ball, with dance, supper and cabaret at a cost of 12s 6d (52.5p).

The years that followed kept to the same opulent pattern, but as the decade wore on it became

Figure 4. In dancing mood. 'Rendezvous' regulars Mr Albert Daykin and Miss Edith Wright (later Mrs Daykin), pictured on the occasion of their victory in the North East Derbyshire Championships in Derby in 1926. Miss Wright, then aged sixteen, was wearing an apple-green dress decorated with pansies. *Photograph donated by Mrs J Clark to Chesterfield Local Studies Library.*

clear that finance was a problem. The novelty had worn off for the more affluent patrons, while the hall's exclusive image deterred the wider dancing public. By 1930 the expense proved too much, and Mr Richardson sold out to a new owner.

Dance Band Days: the 'Rendezvous Dance Hall' 1930-35

His successor, Edwin Morgan, could not have been more different from Mr Richardson. A market trader from Rotherham, he had run dance halls in his native town, and from the beginning adopted a hard-headed business approach. When the hall re-opened in 1930 as 'The Rendezvous Dance Hall', the *de luxe* image was abandoned for a more popular style aimed at the Chesterfield public as a whole. The result was a greatly increased number of patrons, which ensured the financial success of the place for several years. A particularly astute decision by Morgan was his appointment of Syd Murray, who as M C and Floor Manager was to prove a key figure in the successful re-launching of the hall.

On opening night, the response was overwhelming. 700 people turned up to dance to the sounds of the Blue Melody Boys, and subsequent dances drew regular crowds of 350 and 400 a night. Morgan set a relentless programme of dancing six nights a week, with private bookings Wednesday and Friday from 8 pm to 2 am, and dancing from 8 pm to 12 midnight on the other evenings. The afternoon Tea Dances were also retained, and enjoyed the same large attendances. The new-look 'Rendezvous' took off on an incredible wave of popularity that was to last for the next five or six years.

Much of this success was due to Syd Murray, and the resident band, the Blue Melody Boys. The band's regular line-up consisted of (Figure 5) Horace Varley (trumpet), Sid Milner (trombone), Jack Orme and Frank Hubbuck (saxophones), Cliff Turner (saxophone/violin), Lennie Barrett (piano), Jack Evans (bass) and Harold Johnson (drums/leader). One significant change came in 1934, when Jim Lofty took over on bass from Jack Evans, who joined a Sheffield dance band. Unlike the others, Jim was an inexperienced player on his instrument. He eventually mastered the bass and became a valued band member, but he had other useful talents. A capable singer, pianist and music reader, he helped the band's blind pianist Lennie Barrett to memorise new tunes that often had to be learned at short notice. Jim would play them to Lennie, who thanks to his remarkable memory never forgot a tune once he heard it.[12]

Working with the Blue Melody Boys was an exhausting task. The

Figure 5. The Blue Melody Boys in action. *Back row* (left to right): Jim Lofty (bass), Harold Johnson (drums/leader), Lennie Barrett (piano). *Front row:* Sid Milner (trombone), Horace Varley (trumpet), Jack Orme (alto and baritone saxophones, clarinet), Frank Hubbuck (tenor saxophone, clarinet), Cliff Turner (alto saxophone/violin). *Photograph by R Wilsher, Chesterfield Local Studies Library*

musicians would play from 8 pm through to midnight or even 2 am for roughly 2s 6d (12.5p) an hour, and were rarely paid more than 15s (75p) a night. Worse still, they then had to walk home. Jim Lofty had the toughest job, toting his bass all the way from Sheffield Road to Chatsworth Road in Brampton, where he lived with his parents. In spite of this, he recalled his time with the Blue Melody Boys with real affection and pleasure.[13]

Star performer at the 'Rendezvous' was Syd Murray, who organised and supervised the dances. An accomplished dancer, he often demonstrated the latest steps himself, introducing the patrons to the

Palais Glide, Lambeth Walk, Balling the Jack, and the Hokey Cokey. He also organised Treasure Hunts and Fancy Dress dances. A firm favourite with the 'Rendezvous' dancers, he is affectionately remembered by one of his many admirers: 'What a personality he had! Elegant, extremely good-looking and a wonderful dancer. He was our Elvis Presley in those days.'[14]

Syd also introduced Olde Tyme Dancing on Thursday evenings. This became a big attraction, large coach parties regularly making the journey from Sheffield, Derby and Nottingham as well as Chesterfield itself. Syd got the idea from a radio broadcast by Billy Merrin's Commanders, then resident at Nottingham Palais, and booked the band for a one-night performance at the 'Rendezvous' in December 1934. They were such a hit that he persuaded them to stay on for the rest of the week. This sparked an even more ambitious plan. Radio broadcasting was at its height, and most evenings famous London dance bands were featured, recorded live at their various clubs, among them Ambrose, Harry Roy, Carroll Gibbons and Roy Fox. Although the Chesterfield patrons knew of these bandleaders, few had ever seen them perform, and Syd Murray realised what a coup it would be to book some of these 'name' bands at the 'Rendezvous'. He decided to give it a try. Syd started off in a big way, securing Roy Fox and his band, who were touring the Moss Empires in the major cities. Hearing they were to appear at Leicester Hippodrome, he arranged to have a coach collect them at the end of their performance and bring them straight on to the 'Rendezvous'. Roy Fox, the 'Whispering Cornetist', was one of the most popular dance band leaders, and his booking was a tribute to the initiative of Syd Murray, who describes their arrival:

> *They just walked out of the stage door of the Theatre in their stage uniforms on to the waiting coach, and out of the coach straight on to the specially built stage at the 'Rendezvous'. With Roy Fox and his 24-piece band was the greatest crooner of all time, Al Bowlly.*[15]

It proved literally a hair-raising experience for Al Bowlly, who was mobbed by female fans and dragged to the floor. Syd remembered that: 'I had to rescue him as they were plucking hairs out of his head and putting them in their diaries!'[16] Obviously this kind of fan frenzy was happening long before the rock and roll era! Once Al had recovered, the evening was a great success, and from an admission charge of 2s 6d (12.5p) the hall and the band halved takings to collect £89 10s (£89.50p) each. Encouraged by this, Syd Murray arranged further 'name' bookings. The 'Rendezvous' played host to Bertini, resident band at Blackpool's Tower Ballroom,

Frank Payne, Jann Halfini, Lou Preager, Harry Roy and Billy Cotton. They encountered the same enthusiastic response (although perhaps not quite the same as that given to Al Bowlly!)

The popularity of the hall with dancers was phenomenal, drawing patrons from all over the East Midlands. Many romances took place there, and at least eight couples who met at the 'Rendezvous' were celebrating their Golden Wedding anniversaries fifty years later. One man who married in 1935 was so impressed he brought his wife to dance there rather than honeymoon at Blackpool!

This 'golden age' of the 'Rendezvous' was not fated to last. In spite of the enormous popularity of the hall, and the rewards it generated, Edwin Morgan was unsatisfied. In search of more income, he decided to use the 'Rendezvous' as a venue for boxing tournaments which would alternate with the dance nights. The first contests were introduced in 1933, but did not really come into their own until the mid-1930s. By that time, although dances continued to be held, the great days of the 'Rendezvous' were over. Syd Murray tried vainly to dissuade Mr Morgan from the new venture, which he felt would detract from the hall's reputation, and when in 1935 All-in Wrestling was also introduced, it proved the last straw. Syd departed, and the Blue Melody Boys moved on to a residency at the Market Hall. The dancing almost done, the 'Rendezvous' entered a different sector of the entertainment business – the fight game.

Uppercuts and Armlocks: Boxing and Wrestling Venue, 1933-37
It seems Morgan's decision was influenced by two local fighters, Jimmy Conn and Johnny Lowry. Conn acted as doorman at the 'Rendezvous', and Lowry was a frequent visitor. Johnny Lowry was a local boxing hero, former British and Midlands Flyweight Champion with only 10 losses and 4 draws in 234 contests, and had never been knocked out. Partner and co-promoter with Edwin Morgan, he probably set up most of the bouts. Contestants during this period included Billy Gibbons and Sonny Crofts, Kid Kelso and Kid Chocolate, with Jimmy Conn acting as referee. Sadly, the fights were not a financial success, and were cancelled in late 1933. Dancing prevailed through 1934, but at the end of 1935 all-in wrestling was brought in, alternating with the boxing contests.

Best-known of the wrestlers at the 'Rendezvous' was the 'Red Devil', whose real name was Charlie Glover. A former Barnsley collier, he wore red trunks and a red mask which hid his face, and was a favourite with the crowd. Outside the ring he took over as co-promoter from Johnny Lowry, setting up the bouts. He is nowadays better known as the father of the late actor and playwright Brian Glover, who himself wrestled as 'Leon Arras' in later years. Charlie Glover's rivals included Buddy McTaff (aka Atkins), Johanfesson (alias Joe Sheppard) and Karl Tieberman. Mr J R Hudman was a regular attender at the contests, which he remembers as taking place fortnightly on Tuesday evenings in the winter months, starting at 8 pm. Ringside seats cost 2s (10p) or 2s 6d (12.5p) and consisted of wooden forms or chairs; Mr Hudman paid 1s (5p) to view proceedings from one of the balconies, and saw the 'Red Devil' perform:

> *The MC informed us that he would only take off his mask if he was beaten in the bout. In my visits to the 'Rendezvous' I never saw him beaten, but unknown to us at the time of course, the bouts were stage-managed so the longer he kept his mask on the more we flocked for the next promotion.*[17]

Karl Tieberman, short, thickset and shaven-headed, also made an impression. A fair fighter, he was deliberately matched with 'an opponent who tried every dirty trick in the trade, so that the audience were always on Tieberman's side. At the conclusion of the bout he would bow stiffly in Teutonic fashion to the four sides of the ring, and give the Nazi salute.'[18] Another fixture was referee 'Tiger Ted' Baxter, who joined in the entertainment, hurling awkward contestants out of the ring and once accepting a challenge for a bout which he lost, much to the annoyance of the crowd. As Mr Hudman comments, wrestlers and officials could have earned their living on the stage, as well as in the wrestling ring.

Wrestling continued to the end of 1936 with a catalogue of amazing names – Angora the Terrible Turk, Tiger de Lisle, Wild Tarzan, Whipper Billy Watson, Flash Maunders, Tiny Summersgill ('the 7-stone champion of the world'), 'The Mask', Rough-house Rafferty, Rene Labelle ('the Flying Frenchman'), plus Buddy McTaff and the 'Red Devil'. Unfortunately the 'Red Devil', Charlie Glover, caused a serious problem when he was charged with assaulting a British Boxing Board of Control official, John Greaves, while trying to prevent him getting into the hall to check on the licensing of bouts. The case was tried at the Chesterfield Borough Court, which found that neither referee, timekeeper nor seconds were properly licensed, and fined Glover £1 plus costs, binding him over to keep the peace. This damaged the reputation of the 'Rendezvous' but it was now clear Edwin Morgan had made a big mistake in staging boxing and wrestling at the hall. The income was less than he had hoped, and by April 1937 he had sold out his interest.

Figure 6. The Rendezvous Roller Skating Rink. Manager George Jackson with his daughters and staff in the entrance at the opening in 1938. *Photograph donated by the late Mr Robert Ashworth to Chesterfield Local Studies Library*

Wheels on Fire: the 'Rendezvous Skating Rink' 1938-39

On Friday, 11 March 1938 the 'Rendezvous' was re-opened as the 'Rendezvous Skating Rink' (Figure 6). Roller-skating had been popular in Chesterfield since the 1900s, and following the destruction of Renshaw's West Bars venue by fire in 1932, the 'Rendezvous' had the field to itself. The new manager, George Jackson, was a well-known former roller-hockey player, and also a proficient skater and dancer. In 1939 he founded the Spire Rink Hockey Club, whose first practice match on 19 May drew a large crowd. Key players included Cyril Beastall, Renshaw (son of the owner of the West Bars rink), Moody and Emery. Early results were good. Derby Flyers were held 5-5, and Sheffield All Blacks beaten 6-1, Renshaw scoring 4 of the goals, and Spire won the rematch with Derby Flyers 7-5. As a roller-hockey venue the 'Rendezvous' was a success, and matches were well attended. More skating sessions were advertised and hopes for the future were high, but these were dashed by the onset of the Second World War. The rink closed down in December 1939, and never re-opened.

Decline and Fall: 1939-95
The building was converted to wartime use, the old malthouse cellars cleared and renovated as air-raid shelters while the dancehall served local Sea Cadets, and later the Home Guard, as a drill hall and training centre. After the war, workmen from the Borough

Figure 7. The hall, now the Stylax warehouse, in 1992, three years before its demolition. *Brian A Austin Collection*

Highways Department returned to seal up the cellars. In 1947 the building was purchased by Messrs Stockwell and Bax, trading as Stylax. They used the 'Rendezvous' as a bedding factory until 1961, when they leased it to Miss McDowell of Sheffield and then to Waldo Furniture Ltd, who from 1977-87 used the building as a storehouse. Afterwards it was left unoccupied, and in spite of proposals to convert it to a hotel or wine bar, rapidly became derelict (Figure 7). A target for vandals, it was gutted by fire and damaged beyond repair. Soon afterwards, in February 1995, the bulldozers moved in (Figure 8) and the 'Rendezvous' was

Figure 8. February 1995. The bulldozers move in. *Brian A Austin Collection*

Figure 9. Rutland Residential Home under construction on the site, July 1995.*Brian A Austin Collection*

demolished. The site is currently occupied by the Rutland Residential Home (Figure 9).

Nothing now remains of the the building that gave so much enjoyment to so many. The 'Rendezvous' is history. But memories endure, with those who were there, and the younger ones who have heard the stories from those danceband days. For them, the song is ended, but the melody lingers on.

Acknowledgements

This article has its origins in an earlier booklet which I compiled from data and photographs submitted by members of the public and wrote as an information item for the readers of Chesterfield Local Studies Library, and which was later produced in non-commercial form by Derbyshire Library Service. I would like to express my thanks to all the people who contributed information or pictures, several of whom are listed below, and in particular to Mr James Lofty and his daughter Mrs Janet Martin, to Mrs R Ashworth and Mrs Doreen Walker, and to Mrs J Clark for further details on her parents, Albert and Edith Daykin. Thanks also to my former colleague Mr John Lilley for his help in obtaining this information, and also to the Derbyshire Library Service for permission to include this piece in the present volume.

Notes and References

1. Thomas Ward and Richard Hugh Burman, *Map of the Borough of Chesterfield* 1858. Chesterfield Local Studies Library.
2. Ordnance Survey. *Sheet XXV.6.9, ed.1878.* Scale 1:500, from 25″ 1st ed. of 1876. Ordnance Survey; Chesterfield Local Studies Library.
3. *Building plan No.3690, 16 December 1924.* Chesterfield Borough Council.
4. *Derbyshire Times*, 14 March 1925.
5. *Derbyshire Times*, 4 April 1925.
6. *Derbyshire Times*, 29 August 1925.
7. *Ibid.*
8. Marjorie Rawicz, 1989/90.
9. Arthur Hawes, 1989/90.
10. Edith Daykin, 1989/90.
11. *Derbyshire Times*, February 1926.
12. James Lofty, 1989/90.
13. *Ibid.*
14 'Dancers of Yesteryear', 1989/90.
15. Syd Murray, 1989/90.
16. *Ibid.*
17. J R Hudman, 1989/90.
18. *Ibid.*

2. THE DIXONS
AND WHITTINGTON GLASSHOUSE

by Trevor Nurse

The Whittington district lies to the north-east of Chesterfield proper, and comprises three separate areas, namely the villages of Old Whittington, its adjoining neighbour New Whittington to the east, and the district of Whittington Moor slightly further south. All three are now part of Chesterfield Borough, but prior to 1920 they existed as the separate and independent Whittington parish. Old Whittington achieved fame as the location of the Revolution House (then the Cock and Pynot Inn*), where the Earl of Devonshire and his co-conspirators met to organise the 1688 Revolution and the overthrow of James II, while from the nineteenth century Whittington Moor was an area of industrial development centred on the nearby Sheepbridge Coal & Iron Company. Rather less well-known, but equally significant in its day, was the Whittington Glasshouse established by the Dixon family in the early eighteenth century, and which was to prove the parish's main industry for over a hundred years.*

IN 1998 THE LAST OF THE OLD Whittington Glasshouse buildings, known to many as Glasshouse Farm, were demolished. To me these buildings were as much a part of Whittington's history as the more famous Revolution House, although few today would associate the farm with a now vanished eighteenth century industry. The Dixon family who ran the business for over a hundred years rose from glass manufacturers to become wealthy lords of the manor, owning most of the parish and eventually building the spacious Whittington Hall as their residence.

When the first Dixons arrived in Whittington around 1702, the manor lords were the Chaworth family of Annesley Hall in Nottinghamshire. Prior to the arrival of the Dixons, Whittington had usually been owned by absentee lords of the manor who relied on bailiffs to administer their land. The population was no more than 300, half of these living in an area near St Bartholomew's church which is now the old village (Old Whittington), while in the valley of the River Whitting two or three corn mills were in operation. From here the land rises steeply to Grasscroft Wood, the highest point in the Chesterfield district. Richard Dixon built his Glasshouse on this elevated north-east

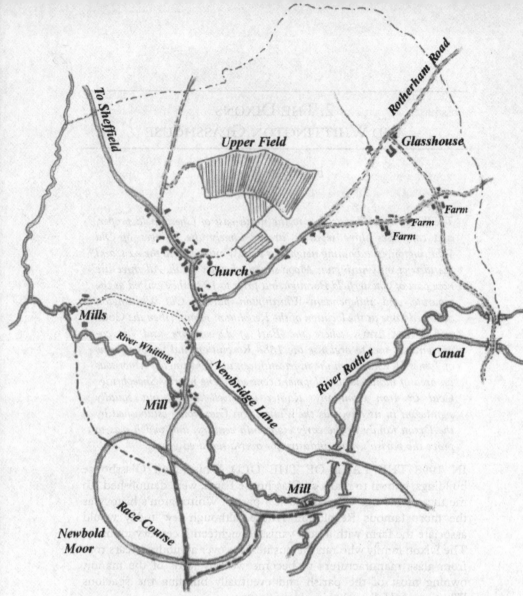

Figure 1. Map of Whittington parish, *c.* 1780-90. *Author's sketch, with additions, from the Enclosure Map*

side of the parish, occupied by a handful of small farms and a couple of cottages on a large common that was mainly scrubland (Figure 1). South of the parish, on Newbold Moor, there may already have been an early form of the racecourse patronised by the Duke of Devonshire and attended by local gentlemen farmers on festive occasions. Through Whittington the Chesterfield – Sheffield road ran past the church and on towards Dronfield further north. The *Cock and Pynot Inn* would have served as a staging post for passing travellers.

Richard Dixon was born *c.* 1660-70 in Worcestershire. Reputedly a fine glassmaker, he came north with his family to work at the Bolsterstone glasshouse near Sheffield, founded by George Fox in 1670. Fox's daughter married one of the Finney family, glassmakers of Stourbridge, who also came north to work at Bolsterstone, and it seems likely that Dixon was an associate of theirs. He worked at Bolsterstone until Fox's death, when he set up his own business. He came to Whittington with his wife Elizabeth and their two sons in the early 1700s, leasing Thorpe Farm which was later to become Glasshouse Farm, and built the Glasshouse near the farm buildings high on the hillside, overlooking the road leading to Eckington, and on from there to Sheffield and Rotherham. This stretch of road no longer exists, having been deliberately replaced by his descendant Henry Dixon with an alternative route, the present-day Handley Road, which was laid in 1825-26.

Richard Dixon was the right man in the right place at the right time. In the early eighteenth century the Sheffield platers were among the finest in the country, producing silver-plated cruet sets and tableware which required fine glass to enhance its beauty, and glass production was a skilled and lucrative occupation.

Why Richard chose this particular location for his Glasshouse remains uncertain. Presumably the open nature of the site allowed for expansion, and was within reach of Sheffield without being close enough to invite direct competition. (Whittington lay just within the boundary of the Sheffield Master Cutlers Company domain, a fact of which he could not have failed to be aware.) For his operation he needed an access road, sand for the glass and coal for the furnace, and apart from the sand Whittington gave him what he wanted, plus a supply of building stone near the farm itself.

The setting up and running of the Glasshouse during these early years must have been arduous work, but by the time Richard died in 1727 he left a well-established business for his son, another Richard Dixon.

Richard Dixon (II) 1690-1736

Richard, the founder's eldest son, married Ann Naylor, daughter of a large Whittington family who lived near the church. The *Poplar Inn* was one of the Naylor houses at that time. Ann's nephew John Naylor was taught glassmaking skills by her husband, and joined the trade. Richard (II) had four sons; Gilbert became Clerk to the Master Cutlers company in Sheffield 1736-77, a useful position for boosting the family business, while William and Richard (III) were both glassmakers. Isaiah, who lived in Eckington and probably worked in Sheffield, was the only son to father children. Richard

Dixon (II) died in 1736 at the young age of forty-six, and was soon followed by his son William in 1743. The result was that Richard (III) took over the works when only twenty-five years old.

Richard Dixon (III) 1718-1769

This Richard appears to have been a bachelor, as no wife appears in any records relating to him, including his will.[1] Short-lived in the family tradition, he survived to fifty and was the last Dixon to work as a skilled glassmaker. Glass production in the eighteenth century was not a particularly healthy occupation. Whether Richard's premature death, and those of his father and brother, were due to its dangers, or to family genetics, remains an unanswered question.

Gilbert Dixon 1713-77, and John Dixon 1742-1816

By the time Richard (III) died the Whittington Glasshouse was a thriving concern, as evidenced in his will, which mentions expenditure on extensions and improvements to the colliery, coal-pits and works.[2] The colliery would have been first used to produce coal for the glasshouse furnace, but later probably became a self-sufficient business of its own. Richard bequeathed the Glasshouse, colliery and coal pits jointly to his elder brother Gilbert and his nephew John, son of Isaiah Dixon. Neither seems to have been involved in glassmaking, and Richard stressed in his will that if they did not wish to carry on the business it should be sold to John Naylor, who was an experienced glassmaker. In 1769 Gilbert was fifty-six and John twenty-seven, and between them they undertook to run the Glasshouse and Colliery; no doubt Gilbert's background knowledge of the cutlery industry proved useful, while the younger John may well have realised the wealth produced from coal and ironstone thanks to the spread of the Industrial Revolution. A further significant local development, the opening of the Chesterfield Canal, was made in 1777, the year that Gilbert died. John then operated as sole owner, at a time when Whittington Glasshouse was producing some of the finest glass in Northern England. From the accounts left by the 'Old Sheffield Platers' it is clear that they bought most of their glassware from Whittington between 1778-1808 (Figure 2.)[3]

Figure 2. Example of Whittington glassware.
Photograph: Trevor Nurse, by kind permission of the owner, Mr Barry Bingham

The Glasshouse must have been a large and diverse operation during this period, making all types of glass and utilising a wide range of skills. Francis Sitwell's accounts at Renishaw show transactions for bottles, varied table glass including cut glass decanters, tumblers, wine glasses, cruets and salt linings, even a chandelier![4]

The Land Tax document of 1780 reveals that John Dixon was not a landowner, but rented or leased a large area from the lord of the manor.[5] This situation was soon to change, as John bought up the land in Whittington as it became available over the next decade or so. He also purchased land in the outlying parishes of Unstone, Dronfield, Brampton and Killamarsh. By 1795 he secured a road to the Chesterfield Canal, in which he held shares, and had a wharf built so barges could tie up and unload; the lock just down from the wharf bears his name. Obviously his glassmaking activities had made him a very wealthy man, but gradually his interests seem to have turned to the lucrative coal and ironstone resources on his land; these made him richer still, but in the process John allowed the Glasshouse operation to decline. 1796-97 saw him lay a tramway down to the canal that linked it with his collieries in Hundall and Grasscroft. Only a mile long, this railway sloped all the way down to the wharf, the loaded waggons running down by gravity and controlled by a brake; the empties were hauled back by horses. The tramway was still in existence in 1880, and the centre of New Whittington was built around it.

The date at which the Glasshouse ceased production is uncertain. It was still producing glassware in 1808, as Watson & Bradley paid £2,000 for glass from 1779 to that year. Sitwells of Sheffield also bought glass from Whittington as late as 1800. In John Dixon's will of 1815, the Glasshouse receives no mention, and probably went out of business *c*.1810-12.[6] At the time of his death at the age of seventy-four, Dixon was lord of the manor, owning two-thirds of the land in Whittington and busy negotiating for more. He had run the Glasshouse for forty years, and proved himself a shrewd and acquisitive businessman. Sadly, he left no heir to his vast estate, both his marriages being childless, and there are hints of a family feud in the will and its inheritance. Oliver Dixon, John's nephew, would have been next in line, but for undisclosed reasons he was barred from inheriting, as were some cousins who were blood relatives. Instead, John chose Henry Dixon, son of his brother's stepson, as his heir. Henry's real name was Offerton, but the family later changed their name to Dixon, often a condition when inheriting a legacy.[7] After

John Dixon's death, his business affairs would presumably have been run by his executors, Joshua Jebb of Walton Lodge and John Haywood of Brimington, but for whatever reason his collieries became derelict within a short time.

Henry was Whittington-born, his parents living near the Glasshouse, but had since moved to Oxford to work as a land surveyor. He didn't return to his home village until 1829 or 1830, after Oliver Dixon had died, and John's surviving widow Ann had only a short time to live. Bearing in mind that both were rival claimants, this again points to family quarrels and ill-feeling over the will. Henry was nothing if not ambitious, and planned to build himself a grand residence. First he had the old Eckington road diverted, replacing it with the present Handley Road, to keep passers-by at a distance from his home. No money was spared on the building, Whittington Hall (Figure 3), a large brick and stone Georgian mansion whose grounds included a boating lake and fishing pond, and a gamekeeper's cottage on the hill; pheasants were bred for shooting on the estate. A lodge stood at the entrance to the long drive, and a head gardener's cottage was built in the grounds at the rear. Henry lived at the hall with his wife Caroline, their children, and his elder sister Elizabeth, and was obviously more interested in acting the country squire than continuing John Dixon's businesses. He had no part in running the Glasshouse, which he leased out as a 240-acre farm to the Cupitt family, and lived on the rents and leases from his tenants. This kind of opulent existence was bound to come to an end, and by 1843 he was clearly having money trouble. Whittington Hall was advertised for sale, but a buyer was not found until 1857, when Henry left and moved to Brandon Lodge, in Leamington Priors,

Figure 3. Whittington Hall, home of Henry Dixon. *Author's photograph*

Figure 4. Dixon family grave in Whittington churchyard. *Author's drawing*

Warwickshire. Here, in 1859, he died, only eighteen months after leaving Whittington.

John and Henry Dixon were the only lords of the manor to live in Whittington, and seem to have had a personal attachment to the place. John in particular owned larger and finer houses elsewhere, but never moved from his works and Glasshouse; he obviously believed in keeping a close eye on the business. His main residence would have been the existing farmhouse, but later a large house was built at the top of the lane near the works, and over the years this was extended several times to form an L-shape. John expressed the wish to be buried in the porch of Whittington church, and for a monument to be erected to himself and his second wife. Unfortunately the old church was demolished in 1863 and the monument was transferred to the new building and later lost (Figure 4).

John Dixon of Brampton Hall

A nephew of John Dixon of Whittington, John came from Leicestershire and inherited land and property in Old Brampton from his uncle. Owner of Brampton Hall and seventy acres, he acquired a coat of arms which he apparently displayed on the doors of his carriage (Figure 5). This is the only known example of local Dixon heraldry.

Figure 5. Coat of Arms adopted by John Dixon of Brampton Hall. *Author's drawing*

The Glasshouse Buildings

So far, no documents have been found relating to the Glassworks, and nowadays no one can be sure of its exact location. The Enclosure Map of 1825-26, shows the buildings quite well (Figure 6), but was drawn fifteen years after production had ceased.[8] The Glasshouse

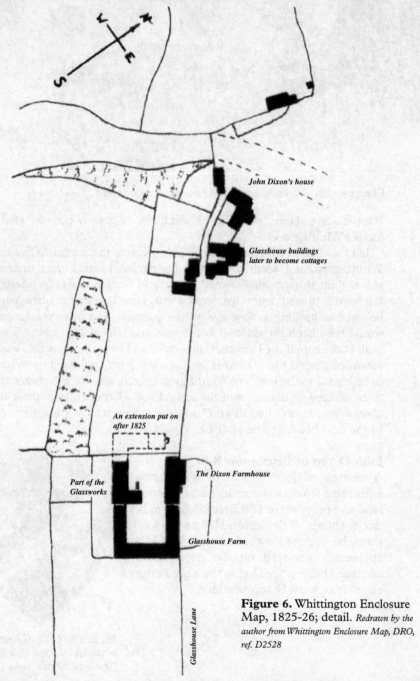

Figure 6. Whittington Enclosure Map, 1825-26; detail. *Redrawn by the author from Whittington Enclosure Map, DRO, ref. D2528*

produced glass for over 100 years, and its furnace would probably have been renovated and may well have stood on more than one site. Similarly, as improved methods of glassmaking were introduced, early buildings may have been altered or demolished, and new structures erected.

The original founder, Richard Dixon, would seem to have lived at Thorpe Farm, and it is likely that he built the furnace and works a short distance along the lane on the right hand side, keeping farm and works separate. The stone steps on the side of the farm led to a large room with one entrance door, probably a store for grain and other food produce (Figure 7). Over the next three generations more houses were built for the extended family, and later on at the peak of production part of the works was brought down and attached to the farm, namely the building opposite the farmhouse. This was a tall structure with windows high up at the side. There was also a square section built out into the yard, which included a glass dome and

Figure 7. Glasshouse Farm buildings. *Author's drawing*

Figure 8. Section with dome and weathervane. *Author's drawing*

Figure 9. Blocked entrance doorway. *Author's drawing*

Figure 10. A glasshouse furnace. *Author's drawing*

weathervane (Figure 8); a floor was later added to make it two storeys. Its large main entrance door, facing down the field, was later blocked and converted to a single door (Figure 9). The weathervane must have been for wind direction, important when firing the furnace. Some residents remember the glass dome, which was demolished during the Second World War.

The furnace was an essential part of the Glasshouse, heating the sand to a high temperature to convert it to glass (Figure 10). No-one

Figure 11. Glasshouse Farm buildings, south view. *Author's drawing*

knows where it was situated, but it would have to be close to the works. In his will, John Dixon refers to the 'pot rooms' near his house.[9] The pots were used in the furnace, and indicate that it may have been somewhere at the top of the lane on the right hand side.

The Cottages

There were five cottages in a yard, the last of the cottages to be demolished in 1938-39 (Figure 11). Situated on the right and looking up the lane, they are still remembered by some, and may have been part of the works. In 1934 there were twelve dwelling houses or cottages occupied on Glasshouse Lane, but by 1940 nothing existed but the farm itself.

Aftermath

The Glasshouse site passed from direct Dixon control when Henry Dixon leased it as a farm to Augustus Cupitt in 1827-28. Cupitt lived there for over forty years, during which time several extensions were made; interestingly, Cupitt was also described in local directories as a brick and tile maker in addition to his farming. One of his extensions, a water tank the size of a small swimming pool, stone-built with a clay lining, is now buried under Mr Ken Hewitt's garden.

Whittington Hall and the Dixon estate were purchased in 1856-57 by William Fowler, principal owner of the Dunston & Barlow (later Sheepbridge Coal & Iron) Company. It then passed to his son Harry Aldham Fowler, who auctioned it off in 1884. The new owner, William Parker, bought the entire estate for £19,000. A man of considerable wealth, his daughter later married the Duke of Somerset. Glasshouse Farm was occupied by his bailiff, Thomas Hughes. Parker stayed for nine years before selling off the estate in lots in 1893. This was the final break-up of the Dixon estate.

Whittington Hall, the Dixon mansion, enjoyed a varied career. Bought by J Morton Clayton of Chesterfield in 1893 for £3,500, it was sold in 1902 to Reverend H N Burden of Clevedon Hall, Somerset. The Reverend leased the Hall for the next twenty-one years as an institution, originally for the care of inebriates, and from 1912 as a mental hospital. A Miss Smith was matron, with thirty staff, and the number of inmates grew from fifty to four hundred.

Afterwards, the Hall continued in existence as a hospital for seventy years, and has recently been sold to a developer who is to build houses in the grounds; the Hall is to be converted to luxury flats.

In April 1998 the Glasshouse Farm buildings were finally demolished, and houses built on the site. In 2002, no trace of the Glassworks or any of its buildings exists. But names like Glasshouse Lane and Glasshouse Common ensure that memory of the Dixons and Whittington's early industry live on.

Acknowledgements

I wish to acknowledge the assistance provided by the staff of Derbyshire Record Office, Matlock, and Chesterfield Local Studies Library. For further information on the Dixons, I am indebted to a present-day descendant of the family, who wishes to remain anonymous. I would also like to thank my neighbour Mr Barry Bingham for access to his copy of Hartshorne's *Old English Glasses*, and for allowing me to photograph the example of Whittington glassware in his personal collection.

Notes and References

1. *Will of Richard Dixon, 2 April 1768*. Obtained by the author from a Dixon descendant.
2. *Ibid.*
3. Bradbury, Frederick, *A History of Old Sheffield Plate*, 1912, rep.1968, Northend Press pp.67-69.
4. Francis Sitwell. Accounts, in: Albert Hartshorne, *Old English Glasses: An Account of Glass Drinking Vessels in England from Early Times to the End of the Eighteenth Century*, 1897, Edward Arnold pp.470-471.
5. *Whittington Land Tax*, 1780, *Q/RE Scarsdale 1780*. Derbyshire Record Office, Matlock.
6. *Will of John Dixon*, 1815. Obtained by the author from a Dixon descendant.
7. *Ibid.*
8. *Whittington Enclosure Map, 1825-26, Ref.D2528*. Derbyshire Record Office, Matlock.
9. *Will of John Dixon*, 1815. Obtained by the author from a Dixon descendant.

3. TRICKS OF THE TRADE:
SOME LEADING CHESTERFIELD ENTREPRENEURS

by David Howes

A GREAT DEAL HAS BEEN WRITTEN by Chesterfield's historians about the Heathcotes, Gladwins, Abercrombies, Foljambes and other eminent families connected with the town, but little if anything has appeared in comparison relating to Chesterfield's leading tradesmen. In their way, leaders of the town's commerce such as John Turner, John Roberts, John K Swallow, James Woodhead and Joseph White are as deserving of honourable mention as their more famous fellow Cestrefeldians. Each of them earned a lasting reputation inside Chesterfield and beyond, and all are still remembered with affection today. It is my intention to focus on three of these men in particular, namely John Turner, J K Swallow and John Roberts.

John Turner was born in Wingerworth in 1826, and grew up in the care of his grandparents at the *Nag's Head Inn* on Derby Road. John's grandparents had built the inn back in the eighteenth century, and it was later to be renamed the *Hunloke Arms*, after the landowning Hunloke family of Wingerworth. In 1828 John's father William Turner took over as landlord of another hostelry, the old *Angel Inn* on Packers Row in the centre of Chesterfield,[1] although he subsequently returned to Wingerworth to take up the duties as 'mine host' at the *Nag's Head*.[2] It seems likely, though, that his brief tenure at the *Angel* marked the start of John's association with Packers Row and with the town of Chesterfield in general.

Below the old *Angel*, at No 9 Packers Row, was the drapery shop of Henry Daniels, while No. 7 housed the coachbuilding business of Peter Littlewood, and at No. 5 stood the premises of the cabinet maker Joseph Eyre (no relation to the better known furniture making Eyres on Holywell Street). As a young man, John Turner served as a draper's apprentice in a shop on the corner of Packers Row and Church Lane. He then left Chesterfield for four years, going to London to further his knowledge of the drapery trade. On returning to Derbyshire in 1850, the twenty-four year old John settled not in Chesterfield but in nearby Staveley, where he set up his own drapery

---

NEW DRAPERY ESTABLISHMENT.

MESSRS. TURNER & LITTLEWOOD

B EG to announce to their Friends and the Public generally, they intend OPENING, in the EARLY PART OF APRIL, the PREMISES now occupied by Mr. EYRE, Cabinet Maker, &c., PACKERS'-ROW, with an Entire New and Fashionable STOCK of GENERAL DRAPERY GOODS, selected from the first Markets in the kingdom.

N.B.—A Respectable Youth as an Out-door APPRENTICE WANTED.

Chesterfield, March 19th, 1856.

Figure 1. Newspaper advertisement for opening of John Turner & William Littlewood drapery store at No. 5 Packers Row. *Derbyshire Courier, 1856*

business in partnership with W K Dutton. After two years the partnership was dissolved, and John Turner continued in business alone.

16 February 1853 was an important day in John's life. On that day he married Mary, daughter of the coachbuilder Peter Littlewood of No. 7 Packers Row. Bride and groom had grown up in the same part of Chesterfield, and Mary may well have been a childhood sweetheart from those early days.[3] The newly-weds settled in Staveley, where their first daughter was born in 1857, but a year before her birth John returned to set up business premises in Chesterfield. In 1856 he and his brother-in-law William Littlewood opened a drapery at No. 5 Packers Row, the building previously occupied by the cabinet maker Joseph Eyre.[4] It was the start of a distinguished commercial career for John Turner in Chesterfield (Figure 1).

By 1872 John was operating as a sole trader at No. 5 Packers Row, and now lived in the town on Brewery Street with Mary, their son and three daughters. He continued trading from No. 5 Packers Row until the 1880s, when he acquired the neighbouring drapery business of Henry Daniels at No 9. The two shops were separated by a yard occupied by the coachbuilder E H Glassbrook; the previous owner had been another brother-in-law of John, G H Littlewood. By 1897, No. 9, No. 5 and Glassbrook's premises were put up for sale by auction.[5] (Figure 2) The bidding began at £5,500 and Turner eventually secured the lots for £7,300. No. 5 and No. 9 continued as separate shops until Glassbrook closed down in 1899 (Figure 3). Not long afterwards his property was used to join No. 5 and No. 9 as a single large store, with an impressive total shop frontage of almost seventy-eight feet. An advertisement in the *Derbyshire Times* for 9

Particulars.

LOT 1.

ALL THAT LARGE

FREEHOLD SHOP AND PREMISES,

Being

No. 9, in Packer's Row, Chesterfield,

Occupied by Mr. John Turner, Draper, and his Undertenants, Comprising:—SHOP and ROOMS, WARE-HOUSES, TWO COTTAGES, PRINTING WORKS, and YARD. This Lot has a frontage to Packer's Row of about **35 Feet** and **10 Inches**, and contains in the whole an AREA of **1,068 SQUARE YARDS** or thereabouts.

The Rent payable by Mr. Turner for this Lot is £140 per Annum, under an Annual Tenancy.

LOT 2.

ALL THAT

FREEHOLD SHOP

Being

No. 5, in Packer's Row, Chesterfield,

Also in the occupation of Mr. John Turner, Draper.

ALSO ALL THAT

FREEHOLD DWELLING HOUSE,

COACH BUILDER'S REPOSITORY, STABLE and COTTAGE,

Occupied by Mr. Edward Glassbrook and his undertenant.

This Lot has a FRONTAGE to PACKER'S ROW of **42 feet** or thereabouts, and contains in the whole an AREA of **1210 SQUARE YARDS** or thereabouts.

The RENT paid by Mr. Glassbrook is £75 per annum under an annual tenancy, and the RENT paid by Mr. John Turner for the SHOP in this Lot is £55 a year under an annual tenancy, making a total annual rental for this Lot of £130. Some of the wooden erections on this Lot belong to the Tenant.

This Lot is sold subject to the rights of light and eaves now enjoyed by Lot 1 as shown on the sale plan.

Figure 2. Page from Property Sale Catalogue (PS106), announcing auction sale of Nos. 5, 7 and 9 Packers Row, 24 March 1897. *Chesterfield Local Studies Library*

Figure 3. John Turner's store, Packers Row, in the 1900s. *Chesterfield Local Studies Library*

March 1901 shows that by then John Turner was trading from greatly increased premises that included No. 5, No. 7, No. 9 and No. 15 Packers Row! The following year, at the age of seventy-six, John Turner retired to private life. In a letter to his many employees he expressed his warmest thanks for the valuable gift they had presented to him, and assured them that he was deeply touched by their kindness and expressions of goodwill.[6]

An active figure in the life of the town, John Turner served on the Chesterfield School Board, where for many years he was Chairman of the Managers. He was also a life Governor of the Chesterfield and North Derbyshire Hospital, having at one time been a member of the Board of Management. In religion he was an ardent supporter of Holy Trinity Church on Newbold Road, and in politics a staunch Unionist. His main form of relaxation, which he indulged for most of his life, was bowls. A keen exponent of the game, he joined the original subscribers to the Chesterfield Bowling Club in 1857. Elected Club President in 1871, he

MR John Turner.

MR. TURNER WAS AS KEEN A BOWLER AS DRAKE EVER WAS.

Figure 4. John Turner cartoon. *Derbyshire Times. 24 June 1911*

went on to serve many times on the committee (Figure 4). His love for the sport was well-known, and he featured in a local press cartoon which had the caption: 'Mr Turner was as keen a bowler as Drake ever was.'[7] Another of his brothers-in-law, George Henry Littlewood, was Club Curator for more than twenty years and following his death in 1890 John took over the post for a time. In 1900, at the age of seventy-four, he was again elected President, perhaps because the club wished to have their longest serving member take their organisation into the twentieth century. In the years that followed he suffered frequent bouts of illness, but was present in 1911 when the Duke of Devonshire, who had been elected Mayor of Chesterfield, was the principal guest of Ye Ancient Bowling Green of Chesterfield at their annual dinner. In his address to the members the Duke paid his own tribute to John Turner:

> *I see we have amongst us tonight a gentleman, Mr John Turner, who was a member fifty-four years ago, and who has known all the presidents personally since that time. I do not know whether the vitality of the Bowling Green is due to such members, or whether their vitality is due to the Bowling Green. I do not suppose Mr Turner will be here for the next fifty-four years, but I hope he will be a member of the Green for a great number.*[8]

John Turner died on 3 August 1913, following a long illness, at the advanced age of eighty-seven. He was then Chesterfield's oldest surviving tradesman and oldest bowler, having been a member of the Bowling Green for fifty-six years, a distinction still unequalled today. In spite of his numerous public works, his greatest achievement remains the long-running success of his store on Packers Row, which had become a permanent fixture in Chesterfield life, and a byword for good service and quality, as well as providing employment for a large number of local people. The John Turner store continued in business for most of the twentieth century before closing down in 1980. The site is now occupied by the Pizza Hut restaurant, but a distinctive Tudor gable remains from the original premises, and dominates the skyline at the end of Vicar Lane. The second floor window bears the name of John Turner, a fitting memorial to one of Chesterfield's most successful sons.

When Burlington Street was opened in 1835, Charles Shaw, a clothier and draper, set up a long narrow shop on the south side of the street. Above the door he erected a beehive sign, and Shaw himself soon became known as 'The Busy Bee'. Shaw was hard up for cash when he started the business, and spent many nights sleeping under the counter of his shop, but eventually succeeded and built up a fortune before retiring to his mansion in Calow. John Kinder Swallow, who took over as new owner of the 'Beehive', may have worked for Shaw beforehand. He kept the shop until 1870, when he sold out to Peter Murphy, who was in business on Glumangate in the town centre. Swallow moved to premises at No. 28 and No. 30 Burlington Street on the north side, and set up a fresh 'Beehive' sign over the door. His new shop duly became the *New Beehive* while Murphy's premises were the *Old Beehive*.[9]

John K Swallow was born in Hepworth, West Yorkshire, in 1822.

He probably came to Chesterfield in the 1840s, working for the clothier Matthew Gibbons in New Brampton, west of the old borough, where both men lived as next door neighbours.[10] He married Frances Martin, daughter of Chesterfield's leading veterinary surgeon Francis Else Martin, whose house and surgery on Holywell Street are now occupied by the Winding Wheel Conference Centre and adjoining shops. The marriage took place at the Independent Chapel, Dronfield, on 18 February 1850, and on the marriage certificate John's occupation is given as draper.[11] Their first child, John Kinder Swallow, was born in the same year, and in all the couple had five sons and three daughters, all of whom bore the middle name Kinder, which may have been John's mother's maiden name. (Interestingly, in the 1851 census John appears not as John Kinder Swallow, but as John Kinder, and is described as a farmer.)[12] He then left Brampton and by 1860 was living in St Mary's Gate in Chesterfield,[13] although all his first five children were born in Brampton, the last being born in 1864. In the 1870s John moved to Low Pavement, and soon afterwards to Thornfield House, Stonegravels, on the north side of the town, where he lived with his wife, five sons, daughter and three servants. By this time he was evidently quite prosperous, employing five men and two boys.[14]

Although there were six other clothiers, tailors and drapers on Burlington Street, Swallow continued to prosper, and by the time of his death on 1 June 1890 had laid the foundations of what was to be the largest department store in Chesterfield. His son, John Kinder Swallow took over with brothers Charles, Frank, Henry and Frederick. Together in the early 1890s they bought Stringfellow and Davenport's hat manufacturing shop, No 32, which stood next door to their premises on the corner of Burlington Street and Packers Row. This building projected several feet into Burlington Street, making the busy area quite narrow and constricted. When Messrs Swallow and Sons decided to pull it down, they offered to sell the projecting piece of land to Chesterfield Corporation in order to bring their new building into line. After some negotiations the Corporation purchased at a price of £1,000, and a new three-storey building was constructed with an exterior of iron, glass and glazed bricks. These last were coloured in ivory, white, green and fawn, and very pleasing to the eye. As the business entered the 1900s, Swallow's added bespoke tailoring and the sale of ironmongery and hardware to their services (Figures 5 & 6).

In 1910 the *Flying Dutchman Inn,* on the corner of Packers Row

Figure 5. Swallow's store on corner of Burlington Street, March 1962. *Photograph by R Wilsher, Chesterfield Local Studies Library*

and Knifesmithgate, closed down and was bought by Swallow's, who installed two large windows and used it as a display area until it was demolished twenty years later. A new three-storey building was then erected on the site, covering two hundred yards. This was of half-timbered construction to conform with the properties on the north side of Knifesmithgate, and while the work was taking place a colonnade was erected which ran the whole length of Messrs Swallow and Sons premises on Packers Row, the shop windows being moved back a distance of six feet. The roof of the colonnade was supported by two rows of

Figure 6. J K Swallow cartoon. *Derbyshire Times, 24 June 1911*

columns, and the shop front was Portland stone, with bronze metal being used for the facia, pilasters and window frames and a granite base. A spacious doorway led in from Packers Row. On Monday, 27 October 1930 a temporary connection was made from the old to the new building, which was later replaced by the new doorway (Figure 7).

Five years after the completion of the new building, a fire threatened to destroy the whole store. It started at 6.15 pm, and but for the prompt action of Miss Gee, an employee, it could have been disastrous. In an interview with the *Derbyshire Times*, Miss Gee stated that she had been round the shop collecting the takings, and had the money in bags in her arms. Entering the hardware department, she saw a glow and sparks behind a curtain, and 'heard a crackling noise':

I dashed to the office and told them to ring the fire brigade. The fire brigade were there almost before we had finished telephoning, but by that time it was impossible to get into the blazing department. While they were phoning the brigade I went back to try and get to the till to empty it, and I fetched two of the men to try and put the flames out with extinguishers but it was useless. The flames were shooting up to the ceiling. They did spread quickly and if we had not given the alarm when we did the firemen would not have been able to save the block.

Figure 7. Swallow advertisement. *Derbyshire Times,* 25 October 1930

Ten minutes later and it would have been too late. The till was found the next morning and the notes inside although scorched and soaking had not been destroyed.[15]

Many of the 120 staff employed by the store had gone home. Those who had not left stayed behind and helped to salvage the stock. At the height of the fire the flames had burned through the roof and were leaping forty feet into the air! After twenty strenuous minutes the fire brigade brought the fire under control.

The last Managing director of Swallow and Sons was John Kinder Swallow (III). He was the youngest son of Frank K Swallow, youngest son of the founder, and was born in 1895. John was educated at Chesterfield Grammar School, Denstone College and Sheffield University. While at Denstone he proved a good rifle shot, and was a member of the School Team at Bisley. At the outbreak of the First World War he joined the Notts and Derbys (Sherwood Foresters) Regiment, serving in France with his battalion from 1915. The following year he was severely wounded, and later won the Military Cross for gallantry after rescuing one of his platoon from No Man's Land while under heavy fire.

After the war he was a prominent figure in the British Legion, and as Chairman of the Appeals Committee helped raise the funds for the Club's headquarters in Glumangate. During the Second World War John served as Head Warden for the West Ward, and in 1946 became a Justice of the Peace, later serving on the Board of Management for Chesterfield Royal Hospital. A keen golfer, he also captained Chesterfield Golf Club and served as secretary for a number of years.[16]

J K Swallow (III) died on 1 April 1957, and two years later his store was taken over by the Macoward Group. During the next ten years they tried to sell, but failed to find a buyer. Swallows' finally closed in 1970, and the following year the building was demolished. After a hundred years in business, the name of J K Swallow vanished from Chesterfield town centre.

The tenure of J K Swallow (III) was also remarkable for the various touring novelty acts and displays it featured over a period of twenty years. Among them were a model of the Sydney Harbour Bridge, a rocket in which children could be seated, a flea circus, and two lion cubs named Vulcan and Vixen. The cubs were on show in cages during the day, but allowed to roam free in the basement at night. Over the six weeks they were at Swallows' they grew rapidly. This was during the Second World War, when staff had to take on fire-watching the store at night. Only brave men ventured into the basement! There were also two midgets who repeatedly recited the same poem all day. One member of staff complained that he had heard their poem so often, he would wake up from his dreams at night reciting it himself![17]

John Roberts, Chesterfield's earliest newspaper editor, began his career not with journalism but at sea, joining the Navy on 8 May 1808 as a volunteer aboard the *Invincible*. He then followed Captain John Hollinworth as a midshipman on the *Resistance*, which was later commanded by Captains Philip L J Rosenhagen and Charles Hole. While on board the *Invincible* he served in the North Sea and at the blockade of Toulon, where a certain Napoleon Bonaparte won fame on the French side. Roberts also took an active part in the defence of Cadiz, where he came into frequent contact with enemy batteries, and witnessed the French siege of Fort Matagorda.[18]

After serving with Captain Hole he returned to England on the *Resistance* under the command of Captain Fleetwood Pellow. He subsequently served aboard the *Devonshire*, at Plymouth in the *Eridanus* under Captain William Paterson, and on the *Minden* where he fought for the flag under Sir Richard King, Commander-in-Chief in the East Indies. As an Admiralty Midshipman he fought with Sir Richard at the Battle of Algiers, where his bravery won him promotion to Lieutenant on 16 September 1816. His last appointments were in June 1817 and February 1819 on *Orlando* and *Malabar,* both ships commanded by Captain John Clavell on the East India station, whence he returned in October 1819.[19]

Roberts came home to Chesterfield, and some years later made an advantageous marriage to Hannah Bradley, the great grand-daughter of Job Bradley, who had been six times Mayor of Chesterfield between 1719 and 1844. Bradley was the town's Postmaster, a position held by other family members, and at the time of Hannah's marriage to John Roberts she was Chesterfield's Postmistress! Significantly, after they were married John took over as Postmaster himself. The Post Office was a four-storey house and shop on the corner of High Street and Packers Row, and is now occupied by a mobile telephone company. Roberts also ran the combined businesses of Bookseller, Printer and Stationer, founded and published the *Chesterfield Gazette*, price sixpence (2.5p). On 26 March 1828 the property was advertised to let, after which the business moved to No 15 High Street, where it remained

CHESTERFIELD
And Scarsdale and

Saturday, April 19, 1828.]   PRINTED AND PUBLISHED BY JOHN ROBERTS, HIGH-STREET,

TO BE LET,

(*Either from Year to Year, or for a term of Years,*)

THE PREMISES now used as a POST-OFFICE, BOOKSELLER'S SHOP, LIBRARY, &c., being one of the best situations for a Retail Business in the town of Chesterfield, consisting of a brick DWELLING HOUSE, fronting both to the High-street and Packer's-row, and with the benefit of a Third Entrance to the Kitchen, &c.

The House consists of four floors, with four apartments upon each floor, exclusive of two separate stair-cases, the same having been formerly used and inhabited as two separate Dwelling Houses, and the merely bricking up two doors would again put it into the same condition, if required,—but it has, for many years past, been occupied altogether as the Post Office, and a Public Library, Bookseller's Shop, and residence for the family. —A very considerable sum has been very lately expended in furnishing new doors, windows, in internal decorations, and a new roof, so that the whole of the Premises are put into a state of the most complete repair;—Water and Gas from the Company has been laid in the most complete manner, for the accommodation of the House and Shop, and the whole will be found to be a most superior situation for any kind of business requiring publicity, contiguity to the Market-place, &c.

Apply at the Office of **MR. THOMAS**, Solicitor, Chesterfield; and to view the premises, to Mr. JOHN ROBERTS, the owner.

SALE THIS DAY.

BUILDING LAND & BUILDING MATERIALS.

TO BE SOLD BY AUCTION,
BY MR. NICHOLSON,

At the House of Miss Johnson, the Angel Inn, in Chesterfield, on Saturday, the 19th Day of April instant, at Four o'Clock in the Afternoon, subject to Conditions to be then produced ;

THE Remainder or South Side of the CLOSE from whence the Reservoir for supplying the Town of Chesterfield with Water was taken, and which South Part of the Close contains 1A. 1R. 16P., and is of Freehold tenure.

At the same time, will also be Sold by Auction,

The whole of the MATERIALS contained in the Buildings between the upper part of the Market-place and the New-square, in Chesterfield, usually called the Old Town Hall ;—the object of the Sale being the removal of these Buildings, and the Land above offered for Sale being a situation selected, where it is considered

Figure 8. Front page of the *Chesterfield Gazette* (later *Derbyshire Courier*), 19 April, 1828, printed and published by John Roberts.

until 1896 (Figure 8.) The last copy of the paper was printed in 1829 when the name was changed to the *Derbyshire Courier*.[20] With its blend of local, national and international news and liberal politics, the *Courier* went on to thrive for almost a hundred years before finally being taken over by its rival, the *Derbyshire Times* in early 1922.

John Roberts died in 1856 and was buried in Holy Trinity churchyard. He had resided at Spital Lodge where his wife Hannah continued to live with the rest of the family until she too died in the 1870s. The business was carried on by their youngest son John Edward Roberts (also a member of the Chesterfield Bowling Club) and by Hannah herself into the early 1860s, when it was taken over by John Ball White. John and Hannah's eldest son, Colonel Henry Roberts, served with the Royal Engineers in the Crimean War, where he supervised the erection of part of the fortifications at Balaclava. His Army career was as distinguished as that of his father had been

Figure 9. Packers Row today. *Photograph by Dennis Middleton*

with the Navy, winning him several decorations and a mention in dispatches. When he retired in 1873 he held the position of Instructor of Fortification at the Portsmouth Naval Depot. Henry's sister Isabel left Chesterfield in the late 1870s and spent many years travelling in Europe. She died in 1906 at her home in Chelsea and

Figure 10. View from Packers Row along Vicar Lane, showing Pizza Hut restaurant with gable from John Turner store. *Photograph by Dennis Middleton*

was brought back to Chesterfield for burial in the family vault at Holy Trinity Church.

Chesterfield has produced many distinguished men and women in the fields of art, science, politics and social welfare, but it is perhaps as well to remember that the town's reputation was founded on its success as a centre of commerce and trade. This is as true today as it was in medieval times, and the entrepreneurs mentioned in this article were among the leading names in local business. Every one is worthy of an honoured memory (Figures 9 and 10).

Notes and References

1. John Turner, obituary, *Derbyshire Times, Derbyshire Courier,* 13 August 1913.
2. Pigot & Co., *National Commercial Directory of Derbyshire*, 1835 p 34.
3. John Turner marriage certificate, 16 February 1853.
4. *Derbyshire Courier,* 19 March 1856.
5. *Property Sale Catalogue,* 1890. Chesterfield Local Studies Library.
6. John Turner, letter, 1902. David Howes Collection.
7. *Derbyshire Times,* 25 November 1911.
8. *Derbyshire Times,*15 July 1911.
9. 'Tatler'(John Pendleton), *Old and New Chesterfield,* 1899, p 52.
10. John K Swallow, obituary, *Derbyshire Times,* 1 June 1890.
11. John K Swallow-Frances Martin, marriage certificate 1850.
12. 1851 Chesterfield Census.
13. 1861 Chesterfield Census.
14. Harrison, Harrod & Co., *Directory of Derbyshire,* 1860 pp 352, 353.
15. *Derbyshire Times,* 30 September 1933.
16. John K Swallow, obituary, *Derbyshire Times,* 12 April 1957.
17. *Ibid.*
18. John Roberts, naval record. Public Record Office, Kew.
19. *Ibid.*
20. Isabella Roberts, obituary, *Derbyshire Times,* 17 February 1906.
21. Pendleton, John, & W Jacques, *Modern Chesterfield,* 1903 pp 34-35.

4. BRAMPTON CHILDHOOD MEMORIES

by John Lilley

TO TELL THE FULL STORY OF BRAMPTON and its history would require a separate book. In the space permitted here, therefore, I have chosen to write about four aspects of Brampton which were part of my childhood – the Pearson Recreation Ground and Wasp Nest Brick Works on Old Hall Road, the Barker Potteries, and the Coliseum cinema.

The Pearson Recreation Ground

Growing up in the late 1930s and 1940s on Old Hall Road, we were very fortunate to be able to play in the nearby Pearson's Recreation Ground. Our back garden overlooked the Ground so it was easy for us to get into it by climbing over the garden wall. Principally it was designed and opened as a children's playground, with swings, a maypole, and a seesaw, and with plenty of grassed space for football and cricket, it attracted many children from the nearby streets and yards (Figure 1).

Figure 1. Pearson's Recreation Ground, April 2002. *Author's collection*

Why 'Pearson'? And when was it opened? According to the Deed of the Ground held by the Borough Council,[1] the land was given to Chesterfield Corporation by the wife of Alderman James Pearson (1853-1905) in May 1913, to be known as the 'Pearson Recreation Ground' in memory of her late husband. James came from the family who owned the Whittington Moor Pottery. He joined the family business with his brother Johnson, but after a disagreement in 1884, James started his own pottery business at Brampton with the Oldfield Pottery at the corner of Walton Road and Chatsworth Road. After his marriage he went to live at Brampton Manor, which he later purchased. He was elected to the Chesterfield Borough Council (which by then included Brampton) in 1892, and three years later was made an Alderman. Whilst on the Council he campaigned for a better water supply for the town. He died in 1905 aged fifty-two, and his wife Helen inherited his estate, which included the Recreation Ground land.[2]

Originally the land was owned from 1861 by the Duke of Devonshire, who leased it to Matthew Knowles, Matthew Henry Knowles and Matthew Wright in 1879. The Knowles family owned the Welshpool & Payne Pottery in Barker Lane, not far from the Ground, which contained beds of Blackshale and Ashgate coal which the lessees were allowed to extract for use at the Pottery. The Duke of Devonshire later sold the land – of 3 acres, 3 roods and 8 perches – in 1889 to James Pearson for £360.[3]

Although I have been unable to find a report on the official opening of the Recreation Ground, it seems to have been laid out and in use by 1914. Mr C P Markham provided the railings and the entrance gate frontage.[4]

Local football clubs began to show interest in the Ground in the late 1920s, and in 1928 Brampton Athletic F C were granted the use of a football pitch. Other applications soon followed from other clubs in the 1930s such as Brampton Gospel Mission F C, Brampton Rangers, and Brampton United, who were granted the use of a pitch for a nominal rent of 5s (25p) for a season (Figure 2).

After the war, in 1947,[5] the Council received a request for local league football to be played on the Recreation Ground and, despite some concerns by the Parks Superintendent of possible nuisance to adjoining residents and danger to children using the playground equipment, it was resolved that, in view of the lack of facilities for playing football in the area, a pitch be marked out and nets be provided. By February 1948 the football pitch was ready and let to Brampton Rovers F C, who regularly played there for several years,

Figure 2. Brampton Gospel Mission FC, 1930s. *Back row:* (left to right) E Hancock, unknown, unknown, E Openshaw, C Hancock, H Courtney, C Simmons. *Front row:* unknown, C White, G Arrowsmith, unknown, E Lomas.
Reproduced by kind permission of Mr Chris Townsend

until moving to another ground.[6] Of course, we played our own football and cricket with the local lads, and some of them showed definite talent. It was very competitive, and kept us fit and out of mischief.

On two sides of the Ground were fairly high stone boundary walls which, over the years, seemed always in need of repair due to damage by vandals. One of the walls bordered the house and orchard of the local doctor, and inevitably kids would climb the wall and raid the orchard. On one occasion the doctor claimed compensation for damage to his fruit trees. In the 1920s damage to the walls and fences resulted in the Chief Constable being asked to have the Ground patrolled, and notice boards appeared, displaying official notices cautioning persons doing damage to walls. I often wondered if anyone was caught doing damage, and forced to pay the appropriate fine.

But one thing we always looked forward to with great excitement and anticipation during the war years of 1941-45 were the visits of the circuses and fairs. The Council readily supported their requests to use the Ground, and it gave Brampton people the chance to see some good professional entertainment at reasonable prices. The circuses that I can remember were Paulo's Royal Circus, Reco Brothers' Empire Circus, Rosaire's Royal Command Circus, Sir Robert Fossett's London Circus & Zoo, and Scott's Royal Circus. The Reco Circus was of particular interest because it featured the Great Blondini in a breath-taking high wire act over the Lions' Den, Rough Riding by the 'White Chief', 'the Only Performing Llama', and the Denvers' knife-throwing act, together with the usual clowns and liberty horses. It was fascinating to see the elephants and horses arriving, and to watch the Big Top being erected with such speed and competence by the circus hands (Figure 3).

The circus visits were usually for two or three days only, but gave two performances a day, a matinee afternoon performance mainly for children, and an evening performance. I remember running back from Old Road Junior School to get a good seat for the matinee at 4.15 pm. Admission prices for children were also cheaper at Matinees, either 7d (3p) or 9d (3.75p), and 1s (5p) for the evening performance. Adults could pay from 1s 6d (7.5p) to 5s (25p).

Much later, in the 1960s, we had two more circus visits. The last, in 1966, was Robert Fossett and George Sanger's Combined Circus

Figure 3. Advert for Paulo's Royal Circus on one of their visits to the Pearson Recreation Ground. *Derbyshire Times, 30 April 1943*

PAULO'S

ROYAL CIRCUS

IS VISITING

CHESTERFIELD (Pearson Recreation Ground, Old Hall Road, Brampton.)

TO-DAY (FRIDAY) & SATURDAY, APRIL 30 & MAY 1st.

For TWO DAYS ONLY   Two Performances Daily at 4.30 and 7.30. Ponderous ELEPHANTS RIDERS ACROBATS MONKEYS DOGS and PIGEONS. WIRE WALKERS Dancing HORSES. MIDGET PONIES EQUESTRIANS ORIENTAL MYSTERIES a HOST of CLOWNS etc. etc. Four Shilling Seats may be booked on Show Ground on day of visit. Free Car Park. Seating Accommodation for 2,000

Admission (inc. tax)—Adults. 1/4, 2/6, 4/-. Children. 7d., 1/4, 2/6. WILL ALSO VISIT CLAY CROSS THURS. APRIL 29th.

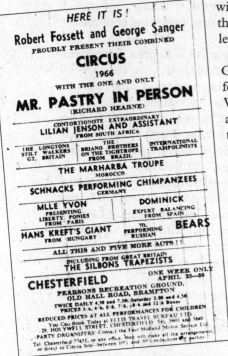

Figure 4. Advert for Robert Fossett & George Sanger's Combined Circus with Mr Pastry at the Pearson Ground, April 1966. *Derbyshire Times, 25 April 1966*

with 'Mr Pastry' (Richard Hearne) as the star attraction, but by this time I had left Old Hall Road (Figure 4).

The one big fair that came to the Ground was Harry Hall's in July 1943, for two weeks. I well remember its Big Wheel and Noah's Ark, the Dodgems and the usual fairground sideshows, the throb of the generators and the music blaring out. In addition, there was the much smaller Children's Fair operated by Mr Day and Mr Sykes.

On visiting the Recreation Ground recently, I was relieved to find that it has changed very little. The original main entrance gates and railings are still intact, but part of the name plate is missing, and it now reads 'The Pearson'. The children's play equipment has been renewed and there are now several wooden bench seats. Sadly, the football pitch seems not to be in use any more (Figure 5).

Figure 5. Name Plate, Pearson Recreation Ground, April 2002. *Author's collection*

Wasp Nest Brick Works

As well as the Recreation Ground, there was another different environment nearby, where we used to explore and play. On the other side of Old Hall Road, opposite Barker Lane, was a semi-derelict brick works with adjacent overgrown tip and quarry. This was known as the Wasp Nest Brick Works. It was fun clambering on the rocks in the quarry and exploring the rock pools which had sticklebacks, newts and tadpoles in them.

There were also two short lengths of narrow gauge rail track which ran from the brickyard into the quarry, and the waggons on the track were still in use. At a distance, we would watch the empty waggons coming down one track and filled waggons returning on the other to the works. Presumably they carried the coal and clay extracted from the quarry. Occasionally the rocks had to be blasted with explosives. It is not clear when the brick works were built, but directories, maps and Council Minutes suggest that it was around 1909, and by 1912 the Wasp Nest Brick & Tile Company was firmly established on the site with the brick kilns, chimneys, quarry and rail track all in place.[7] The joint owners were two local builders, Edward Silcock and Edwin Hattersley, a joiner, Arthur Heath, and a butcher, Arthur Gibbons. No doubt the two builders were responsible for the erection of the brickworks, and with a ready supply of bricks they built much property in Chesterfield. Edward Silcock in particular built the houses in Chester Street, Bank Street and Hope Street in Brampton, and two well known landmarks, the chimney stacks at the Electricity Works and at Robinsons' Wheatbridge Mills.[8]

The Wasp Nest Brick Company ran the business until around 1934, when it seems that a newly formed company, The Chesterfield Brick Co (1934) Ltd took it over. Brick-making ceased in the mid-1940s when the firm closed down. There must be many houses in and around Chesterfield built with Waspnest bricks. I still have a few at the bottom of my garden with the name 'Wasp Nest' imprinted on the side of them.

I have a particular interest in the brickworks because my great-great-grandfather, Joseph Lilley, was a master brickmaker who came from Warwickshire to Brampton with his family *c*. 1844-45, and for a short time lived in one of the old Wasp Nest stone cottages close to the works. Two of his sons also became brickmakers who, like their father, worked at other brickworks in the district.

Next to the brickworks was the Inkerman Pool, created when the former nineteenth century Inkerman Colliery workings were flooded with water after closure in the early 1900s. The overgrown spoil heaps around the pool reminded us of the coal-mining of the past.

The pool was used for swimming by Chesterfield Swimming Club, which had its own changing huts and diving board (Figures 6 & 7). Because of the steep sides to the pool, some of the Brampton lads used to dive in off the top of the banks. Some local fishermen could be seen trying their luck in the waters, but I never saw them catch anything! The pool was said to be very deep, and unfortunately a few drowning tragedies occurred.

Above the pool on the Ashgate side was the derelict pottery building with its chimney, of the former Ashgate Pottery Co Ltd. This pottery was formerly noted for its making of pots and pancheons.[9] It is interesting to note from the Ordnance Survey maps of 1898 that, in addition to the Inkerman Colliery, there was also the Inkerman Brick Works run by the Chesterfield Brickmaking Co Ltd, on the site of the later Ashgate Pottery. Little is known about the brickworks or the pottery, but in 1901 the Chesterfield Brickmaking

Figure 6. Swimming at the Inkerman Pool in the 1920s. The Ashgate Pottery and chimney are on the left of the picture. *Chesterfield Local Studies Library.*

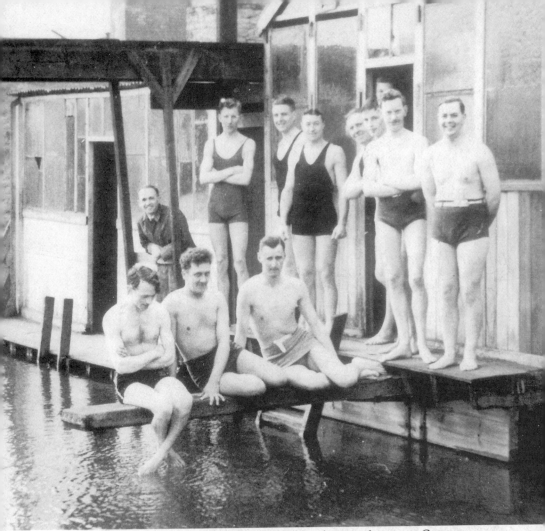

Figure 7. Inkerman Pool in 1937. Among the swimmers shown are, George Courtney (seated, 2nd left), Frank Harding (seated, 3rd left), Harold Turner (standing, 3rd left) and Dickie 'Bunny' Unwin (standing, far right). *Photograph donated to Chesterfield Local Studies Library by Harold Turner.*

Co Ltd went into liquidation, the brickworks closed and was probably converted for pottery making. Presumably the coal extracted from the colliery was used at the brickworks, but by 1914 the colliery had been abandoned.

Soon after the war, about 1946-47, the Council built pre-fabricated houses on the tip and adjacent field, and extended Churston Road to Old Hall Road. Later the brickworks were demolished, the quarry filled in, the Inkerman Pool drained and filled, and the whole site redeveloped for housing around 1969-70, including a large children's playground and football pitch.[10]

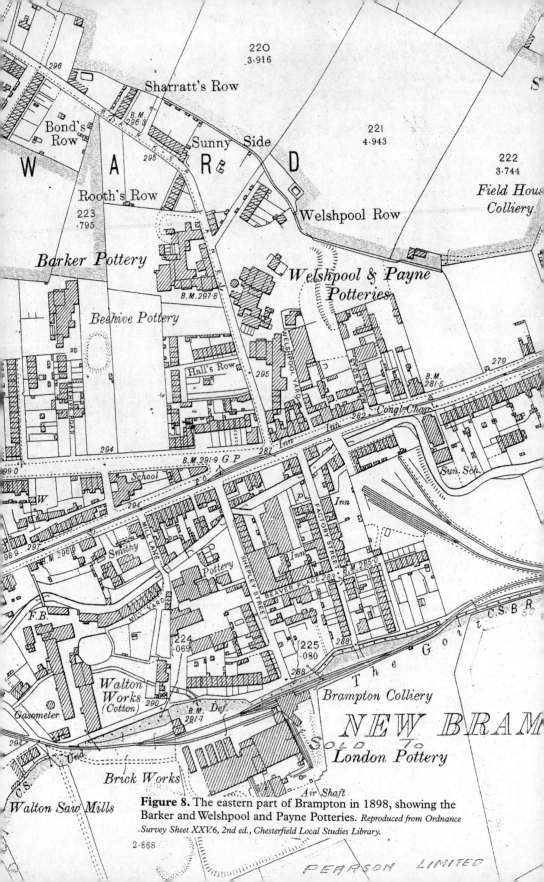

Figure 8. The eastern part of Brampton in 1898, showing the Barker and Welshpool and Payne Potteries. *Reproduced from Ordnance Survey Sheet XXV.6, 2nd ed., Chesterfield Local Studies Library.*

The Barker Lane Potteries

I have already mentioned the Welshpool & Payne Pottery near to where we lived. Opposite this pottery, on the far side of the road, was the Barker Lane Pottery, which we could see from our house and from the Recreation Ground. Its 140 foot tall chimney was close to the boundary fence, and made its presence felt when it was fiercely billowing out smoke. This may have been a pleasing sight to some, but not on Monday wash days!

Chesterfield was well known for its potteries, whose success was due to the readily available coal and clay in the district, and the demand for stoneware products. At one time there were ten potteries in Brampton alone, including the Ashgate Pottery (Figure 8). By 1940 the Barker Pottery was the only one in operation, the rest having closed down in the four decades after 1900. Barker was established in 1828 by Samuel and Henry Briddon, who had already founded the Beehive Pottery in nearby Beehive Yard, and took its name from the Barker family of Bakewell who owned the land on which it stood. No doubt it was the Brampton fireclay that caused the potteries to spring up in Brampton, because of its superior quality, which enabled excellent ware to be produced from it. Barker used to get its clay from a field opposite the pottery, and other clay sites in the area before extracting from Orwin's pit at Newbold, and latterly from the Brockwell pit which had the best quality clay. Some of the houses on the east side of Old Hall Road are built on the site of clay holes. Many pottery owners also owned coal pits, or leased land to extract coal. The Briddons owned the Brockwell pit near to Ashgate Colliery, and also leased land with Luke Knowles at Spital to extract more coal. After the Briddons finished, Barker got its coal from the Turnoaks pit, which it co-owned with two other pottery masters.[11]

In 1881 Samuel Briddon sold the firm to Mr George Shaw, a colliery owner from Sheffield, who formed the Barker Pottery Company. A description of the pottery in 1899 referred to its

well-equipped works on a considerable area of ground. The plant is completely up to date with all the latest improvements in pugging mills, throwing wheels and other appliances of the trade, and includes a range of seven kilns, two round and five long ones. There are several drying sheds heated by stoves and a large warehouse and packing room.[12]

By 1914 Mr Shaw's son, another George, had taken over the business and bought Knowles' Welshpool & Payne Pottery across the road. As both potteries made much the same type of Brampton ware,

Figure 9. Workers at the Welshpool & Payne Pottery (M Knowles & Son), Barker Lane, in May 1928. *Chesterfield Local Studies Library*

Figure 10. Inside the Welshpool & Payne Pottery (M Knowles & Son). *From the 'Illustrated Guide to Chesterfield', 1899, reproduced by kind permission of Alan Hill Books, Sheffield. Chesterfield Local Studies Library*

it was probably no surprise when they merged. Both were reconstructed and brought further up to date.

The works of Messrs M Knowles & Son which were known as the Welshpool & Payne Potteries, were among the largest in Brampton. They embraced the old works carried on during the eighteenth century by Mr Blake and afterwards by his widow, and those of Luke Knowles, with considerable additions. They passed into the hands of Matthew Knowles around 1840, and were further enlarged by him. Later he was joined in partnership by his son, Matthew Henry Knowles, and the works were again enlarged in 1875. The many varieties of brown and stoneware goods were made for the Australian, Russian, African and Jamaican markets as well as for the home trade(Figures 9-10).[13]

The stoneware and brownware products, many of which can still be found in local homes, included jam jars, tobacco jars, puzzle jugs (often with greyhound handles), posset pots, candlesticks, flower pots and vases, fountains, pudding dishes, moulds, teapots, footwarmers, spirit merchants' bottles, ginger beer bottles, stew-pots and cooking dishes. What were once everyday utensils have now become 'collectables.' Barker's leading line in stoneware was their special make of filters, fitted for use in sizes from one to six gallons capacity, and for which there was a ready market, not only at home, but also in France, Germany, South Africa, China and South America.

In the 1930s during a trade recession, the pottery managed to keep its sixty employees moderately busy, and a new bulldog trade mark was introduced for its Barker Ware, denoting strength and reliability. However, by the mid-1950s competition from glass and plastics, which had affected the industry for some time, resulted in a drop in demand for its wares, and despite the installation of modern machinery at the pottery, it was unable to meet current needs. Orders dwindled, and after 129 years of pottery making, it closed in November 1957.[14]

The two potteries were demolished in 1961 and replaced by bungalows, an office block, and a car repair centre. Some of the pottery owners built houses for their workers, and Welshpool Place on Barker Lane, with its eight original cottages, still survives today as a reminder of the pottery and its workers. But that's not quite the end of the story, because pottery making is now back in Brampton! A local potter, Janine Marrion-Jones, has recently opened a shop and pottery, JMJ Pottery, on Chatsworth Road. She makes domestic stoneware in the Brampton Ware tradition but using colourful modern glazes.

Brampton Coliseum Cinema

Our local cinema on Chatsworth Road, next to the Brampton Brewery, was the Coliseum, and no doubt many people have memories of it during its fifty years, so it seems appropriate to look at its history. When the Mount Zion Primitive Methodist Church, built in 1827, closed in 1906, and its members moved to a newly built church further up the road, the old Chapel was taken over by Charles Senior and his family who converted it into a cinema, opening on 7 October 1907. They left the iron railings along the front *in situ*, and converted a watchman's hut into a paybox. The first programme, advertised as 'Animated Pictures', had more than a dozen items with songs and cello solos between the films. Mr Norman Grey played the piano, whilst Mrs Senior gave violin solo recitals during the reel changes. Other acts are also said to have appeared. Up to 1915 the cinema was advertised as the Central Hall (Figure 11), but by then owned by Whitham, Blank & Co. By 1916 Mr A P Blackham was the manager, the building had undergone refurbishment and was now known as the Brampton Coliseum Picture Palace. Mr Blackham later became the proprietor, and he had engaged Mr R G Bates as resident manager by 1920. At this time the cinema had 900 seats, with prices from 4d (1.33p) to 1s (5p).[15] The Coliseum changed hands again in the mid-1920s, the new owners being a company called Entertainments (Chesterfield) Ltd, who by 1928 had reduced the price of the dearer seats to 9d (3.75p).[16] People remember the silent pictures, with the pianist keeping time with the 'cliff-hangers' in front of the screen. Words were put on the screen to help the audience follow the picture. I remember my mother telling me that she occasionally played the piano for the silent films at the Coliseum. I knew that as a girl she had piano lessons in the 1920s, but I was not aware of her cinema-playing talents.

In the early 1930s, the Coliseum seems to have had a

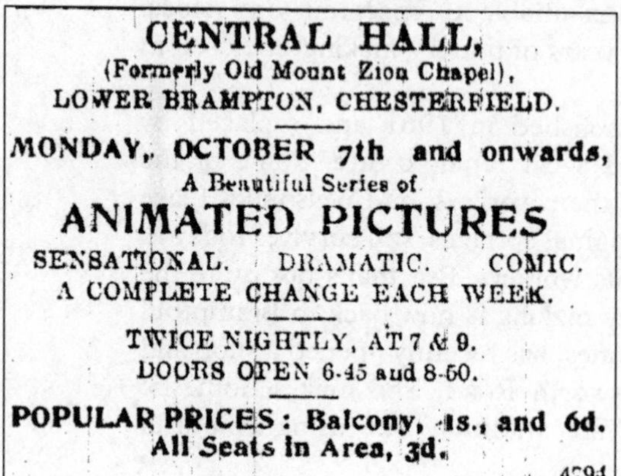

> **CENTRAL HALL,**
> (Formerly Old Mount Zion Chapel),
> LOWER BRAMPTON, CHESTERFIELD.
>
> ────
>
> **MONDAY, OCTOBER 7th and onwards,**
> A Beautiful Series of
>
> ## ANIMATED PICTURES
> SENSATIONAL.   DRAMATIC.   COMIC.
> A COMPLETE CHANGE EACH WEEK.
>
> ────
>
> TWICE NIGHTLY, AT 7 & 9.
> DOORS OPEN 6·45 and 8·50.
>
> ────
>
> **POPULAR PRICES : Balcony, 1s., and 6d.
> All Seats in Area, 3d.**
>   4794

Figure 11. First advertisement for the Coliseum cinema, then the Central Hall, October 1907.
Derbyshire Courier, October 1907

varied life. Some adverts appeared in the press, and it was said to have often been closed for a while. A serious fire in February 1939 destroyed part of the building, but after extensive internal reconstruction at a cost of £6,000 it re-opened on 30 October 1939 with the film *Boys' Town* starring Spencer Tracy and Mickey Rooney. It had a new foyer, carpeting, lighting, and the latest B T H sound equipment. Seating was increased from 400 to 600 including a small balcony, and to allow every member of the audience to have an unrestricted view of the screen the ground floor dipped in the centre instead of a steady slope to the front. Three matinees were introduced on Mondays, Wednesdays and Saturdays, with continuous evening showings from 5.30 pm to 10.00 pm. Stall prices were 4d (1.33p) and 6d (2.5p), and the balcony 9d (3.75p) and 1s (5p).

During the war years seats remained at reasonable levels, and films were shown six months behind the Circuit cinemas of the town. 'Cowboy' films seem to have run well here. My favourites were the *Tarzan* films, Old Mother Riley, Laurel and Hardy, and the Norman Wisdom comedies. In 1950 seats were priced from 10d (4p) to 1/9d (8.75p), and by 1955 the cinema was advertising 'the new curved Panoramic screen' for the films *Desert Song* and *Calamity Jane*.

However, with business declining, a rise in running costs, and high Entertainment Tax, the Coliseum closed on Wednesday, 30 October 1957, the last film shown being *High Society* with Bing Crosby, Grace Kelly, Frank Sinatra and Louis Armstrong. The building then fell into disuse, later becoming a store and warehouse, and eventually – in the late 1970s – part of a car showroom.[17] Like the potteries and so much of old Brampton, the Coliseum is no more, but half a century later those childhood memories are still with me, and they will never fade.

Acknowledgements

Sincere thanks to Alan Hill Books, Sheffield, for permission to reproduce the Knowles Pottery photograph from their reprint of *An Illustrated Guide to Chesterfield;* Robert Hattersley and Ken Silcock for information on their respective grandfathers; and to Chris Townsend for his kind loan of the Gospel Mission F C photograph.

Notes and References

1. *Deeds of Pearson Recreation Ground,* Chesterfield Corporation Deed Box No 72, Parcel No 23, Chesterfield Borough Council.
2. Pamela Wass, *The Potteries of Chesterfield* (study, Hons Art, Craft & Design, University of Sheffield), 1989 p.51, Chesterfield Local Studies Library.

3. *Ibid.* p.38.

4. T P Wood's *Almanac*, 1916 p.302, Chesterfield Local Studies Library.

5. Chesterfield Borough Council, *Minutes December 1946-October 1947*, No 3234 p.1232, No 3496 p.1311, No 4304 p.1612, Chesterfield Local Studies Library.

6. Chesterfield Borough Council, *Minutes December 1947-November 1948*, No 1572 p.573, No 2990 p.1101, Chesterfield Local Studies Library.

7. Kelly & Co, Ltd, *Derbyshire Directory*, 1912 p.119: *Ordnance Survey Sheets XXV.5, XXV.6*, eds of 1876, 1898, 1914 (Scale: 25":1 mile), Chesterfield Local Studies Library.

8. Robert Hattersley & Ken Silcock, personal reminiscences.

9. Robinson & Sons, *The Link Magazine*, No 160 March 1958 p.36, Chesterfield Local Studies Library.

10. Chesterfield Borough Council, *Minutes December 1946-October 1947*, No 3006 p.1143, No 3432 p.1291; Minutes December 1947-November 1948, No 1230 p451, Chesterfield Local Studies Library.

11. Pamela Wass, *The Potteries of Chesterfield*, p.38, Chesterfield Local Studies Library.

12. Chesterfield Borough Council, *Minutes December 1946-October 1947*, No 3294 p.1215, No 3737 p.1364, Chesterfield Local Studies Library.

13. *Derbyshire Times*, 9 April 1932 p.17.

14. *An Illustrated Guide to Chesterfield*, 1899 p.35, Chesterfield Local Studies Library.

15. Pamela Wass, *The Potteries of Chesterfield*, 1980 p.38,Chesterfield Local Studies Library.

16. Robinson & Sons, *The Link Magazine*, No 160, March1958 p.36, Chesterfield Local Studies Library.

17. Brian Hornsey, *Ninety Years of Cinema in Chesterfield*, 1992 p.5, Chesterfield Local Studies Library.

18. *Ibid.*

19. *Ibid.* p.6.

5. I Remember Arkwright

by Charles Dickens

Editor's introduction

The former mining village known as Arkwright Town lies three miles to the east of Chesterfield on the Bolsover Road, between the neighbouring districts of Calow and Sutton-cum-Duckmanton. The present-day village is new, its buildings erected in the 1990s on the opposite side of the road from the original settlement following a methane leak that endangered Arkwright and its inhabitants; the huge opencast mining development begun during the same period by British Coal and continued by R J Budge, is still in operation. The earlier village was itself of fairly recent duration, begun as a cluster of houses around a railway station on the Lancashire Derbyshire & East Coast Railway line founded in the 1890s by William Arkwright of Sutton Scarsdale Hall to transport coal from his mines to Chesterfield and beyond. (An 1899 trades directory comments merely that 'the Lancashire, Derbyshire and East Coast Railway has a station here called 'Arkwright Town'') Later growth centred on the sinking of Arkwright Colliery by directors of the Staveley Coal and Iron Company in 1938, part of North Derbyshire's thriving coal-mining industry. The pit closed fifty years later in 1988.

Charles Dickens lived much of his early life in Arkwright, and returned to work for several years as a miner at the colliery. Here he records some of his more lasting memories.

I WAS BORN ON 30 MARCH 1940 IN ARKWRIGHT TOWN, and christened Charles William Dickens after my father's brother, Uncle Charlie. At that time Arkwright was a close-knit, self-sufficient mining village which was mainly made up of five rows of terraced houses (Figure 1). Chesterfield Road (Figure 2) faced on to the main road from Bolsover, that passed the village on its way to Calow and Chesterfield. The other rows were Hardwick Street and Penrose Street, both of which were divided into two separate rows of houses. We lived at No 52 Hardwick Street, in the last row near to the *Station Hotel* (Figure 3). In addition to the terraced rows there was a detached house in its own grounds that belonged to Mr Perrins, who

Figure 1. Ordnance Survey. Sheet XXV N E, 1921 ed. Scale 1:10560; 6"- 1mile. *Ordnance Survey, Chesterfield Local Studies Library*

Figure 2. Chesterfield Road, Arkwright, as approached from Calow. *Edwin Rotherham Collection*

Figure 3. Hardwick Street. No. 52, Charles Dickens' birthplace, is towards the end of the road on the right. *Edwin Rotherham Collection*

was a plumber by trade, and two sets of cottages. Three of these stood close to Mr Perrins' house, the other three being next to the Social Club. Today Mr Perrins' house is the only building left standing of the Arkwright Town I knew as a boy.

Arkwright had its own amenities, with a public house (the *Station Hotel*), Miners' Welfare Club, five shops plus a fish and chip shop, a school and school house, a youth club and a chapel which was later used as a doctor's surgery (Figures 4 & 5). It had its own playing field, and across the road was a caravan site and allotment gardens where the Arkwright villagers grew their own vegetables. The colliery stood on Sutton Lane off the main road, and when I was young there was also a railway station. I remember taking trips to Skegness by train as a boy, but passenger services stopped before I left school, and the railway fell into disuse. But with four Corporation buses running to Chesterfield every hour, you couldn't say we were cut off from the outside world. Most of the men in the village worked at Arkwright Colliery or neighbouring pits, and there were some who worked at Chesterfield in the engineering factories like Markhams or the Chesterfield Tube Works, or Robinsons packaging firm on Wheatbridge Road.

My father, John Thomas Dickens, worked for the Staveley Coal & Iron Company. Before that he'd had twenty-one years in the Army, and he was a strict disciplinarian, but I always found him to be fair. My mother, Beatrice, was a homely person who like many other women in the village didn't go out to work. She had plenty to do running the home and looking after me and my sister Maureen. I also had an older stepbrother, but I didn't find out about him until much later. He was seventeen years older than me, his name was Colin Dyson. Apparently he and my father didn't get on, and Colin had joined the Army. He later married and lived away from Arkwright, and after my father died we got to know each other quite well.

When I was growing up in Arkwright you couldn't just wander off as you liked. Everybody knew everyone else, so any misdeeds were soon reported back, and then there'd be trouble. You were always expected to be home at tea-time, and when you'd eaten your meal you had to sit at the table for a further ten minutes to ensure that you'd properly digested your food. Anyone older than us was addressed as 'Mr' or 'Mrs', and adults had to be shown proper respect. I suppose you'd call it a strict upbringing nowadays, but I don't think it did us any harm.

Arkwright School stood at the top of the road on Chesterfield

Figure 4. Former Post Office, Fish and Chip Shop and Grocery Store. *Edwin Rotherham Collection*

Figure 5. Miners' Welfare Club. *Edwin Rotherham Collection*

Figure 6. Arkwright School. *Edwin Rotherham Collection*

Road (Figure 6). It was a large two-storey building, and catered for both primary ('juniors') and secondary ('seniors') pupils. On my first day at school, my mother took me to the school gates, and as soon as she let go of my hand I ran away. From what she told me I was running around Arkwright for about three hours with them chasing me. Mr Watkinson, a neighbour of ours, was the one who caught me in the end, and that wasn't until eleven o'clock! Mind you, I was punished for it once I got home, and I didn't do it again. For all that I had Charles Dickens for a name, I can't say I was much of a scholar while I was there, although after that first episode I didn't cause too much trouble. The lessons were there to be done, and I did them, but I never really was very interested, and no particular subject caught my fancy. Apart from sport, of course.

In fact, the main incident that comes to mind from my time at school is one day in the winter of 1947, when I was seven years old.

That was a bad winter, and anyone who remembers will tell you the same. In Arkwright we had a heavy snowfall with drifts that stood six feet high in places. I came home from school through the snow, and once I got home I started to pull off my Wellington boots. Unfortunately for me, I slipped and fell, and my left leg went straight into a bucket of red hot water that my mother was using for the washing. I scalded my leg badly, and apart from a lot of pain it meant I had to be taken to Chesterfield Hospital. I had to make several trips there before my leg healed properly, and each time my father had to carry me on his shoulders through the snowdrifts and all the way into Chesterfield. Thinking back, it must have been a tough job for him. Not that I enjoyed it very much either.

As a child I was never short of friends. I grew up playing with the rest of the lads in the neighbourhood, and when we were young most of our games were played on the street. We'd play marbles or hopscotch, whip and top, skipping, and a game we called 'husky fusky, finger or thumb', where all but one of the players bent over in a line against the wall. The one who wasn't in the line would call out 'husky fusky finger or thumb', and hold up either his finger or thumb, and you had to guess which. If you got it right, it was your turn to ask the question. Another pastime of ours was flying kites. We made our own kites, from two crossed sticks with brown paper wrapped around them. We used plain flour and water as our glue to stick them together. Some of those kites of ours were pretty big, maybe three feet by two, and it was quite something to see them flying. On Saturday mornings we'd often go to the cinema, either in Chesterfield or maybe in Bolsover, the nearest town on the other side of Arkwright. Apart from that, we did a lot of walking, going on long strolls out to Calow, or Sutton-cum-Duckmanton. It didn't cost us anything, and we made sure we enjoyed ourselves. I can't say I was a regular churchgoer, but before the chapel became a surgery I remember going on weekday evenings to something called Sunshine Corner, where we had a kind of religious service, with a sermon and hymns and songs (Figure 7). There was a special song they had, and it started off with 'Sunshine Corner, all is very fine...'. Something like that. I can't remember too much else about it.

All the lads loved sport, especially football, and I was no exception. What I liked best about school was the Sports Days, and playing in the school team. I played in the junior side from the age

Figure 7. Former Chapel, later doctor's surgery. *Edwin Rotherham Collection*

of eight, and moved on to the seniors when I was twelve. The reason we liked Sports Day so much was because it gave us another chance to play football. We played cricket too, but for some reason that never seemed to catch on with the lads as much as football did. With playing together so often, we soon had a good understanding of each other's abilities, and had a good team. Arkwright played against other school teams, and usually did quite well. We were always disciplined, and our teachers were strict like most in those days, but it didn't stop us enjoying the games.

The playing field was at the bottom of the village, out beyond the railway station, and we'd be down there seven nights a week. Playing football, of course. What else? It didn't stop when we left school, either. The year before I left, when I was fourteen, I joined the Youth Club side that was run by a Mr Len Barber. He took the job very seriously, entering us in a proper league competition and making sure we trained on the playing field every week. Several of my friends were in the same side, and we more than held our own against the other sides. In fact, the team became so popular that we had to hire a bus for our fans to follow us to the away matches. I remember one game we played away against Barlborough. They had a strong side, with a goalkeeper who later went on to play for Chesterfield, and at that time they hadn't been beaten at home for three years. We won that game 2-1, and you should have seen their faces! They were so desperate not to lose to us that the keeper came out and played centre-forward for the last twenty minutes, in the hope of getting an equalising goal!

I heard that our playing field had been a gift to the village from William Arkwright, who lived at Sutton Scarsdale Hall years ago, and laid the railway line into Chesterfield that Arkwright grew up around. Later on there was some trouble over who owned it, and a farmer claimed it was his land. I think he must have got it eventually, because in the 1960s we trained and played on a couple of fields in Calow, not far from the cenotaph on the left side of the road from Arkwright.

After the Youth Club it was on to the village team, Arkwright F C. I was seventeen then, and working at the pit, but the football didn't stop! My usual position was left-back or left-half, but in this team I was really up against it. We had so many good players there were first and second elevens, and I could never break into the first team. Several of the first choice Arkwright players went on to higher things. Mansfield Town were interested in two of them, but they backed out when the Arkwright manager wanted more money. Some of the players I remember from that time were Michael Greenall, Trevor Rason, Brian McCann and the Henson brothers, Sammy and Barry. The regular centre-forward was Gren Jepson, and I used to think he was one of the best local centre-forwards I'd seen. A real Denis Law type, he could score with his back to goal. He had trials with a First Division club, and scored seven goals, but for some reason he never followed it up. Probably money, there weren't the same rewards in those days that there are today. The saddest one was Albert Bryant, a nippy little outside-right, who always impressed me when he played. Once he got past you on the wing, he couldn't be caught.

Albert was due for a trial with a league club one Saturday, and on the previous Wednesday he changed shifts with a friend to work on the pit top at Arkwright Colliery. He was crushed between two trucks and killed. It was a tragic waste of a real footballing talent.

I left school in 1955 with no examination qualifications to my name, and applied for a job at Arkwright Colliery. I did my six months training at Grassmoor Training Centre, but at that time Arkwright had no vacancies for jobs underground, so I worked at the pit top on the screens. The job was to pick out the rubbish and separate it from the coal as it went past you on the screen, 'bat scratching' the miners called it, and it was no easy task. My arms were going like a humming bird's wings at times! After a while I got a transfer to Markham No 2, which was at Duckmanton next door to Arkwright, where I worked on what they called the 'materials', with a pony and tubs. My job was to harness the pony to the loaded tub and take them through to the underground roadways we called 'gates'. You had to stay alert, as sometimes in tight spots between the doors the pony would rear and jump, and kick out with its hooves. All you could do then was make sure you kept clear of it, and waited for it to calm down before carrying on again. After a year or so, I moved on to a similar job at Markham No 1. At this pit the job was automated, with a mechanical hauler drawing the tubs to the coal face, and I had to clip the tubs to the ropes. You didn't have the pony to watch out for, but this job had its own dangers. If someone decided to run the roller while you were still clipping the rope, you could end up getting tangled in the ropes and pulled into the machinery, so it didn't pay to lose your concentration.

I left the pit after I was eighteen-years-old, and joined the Army with a friend of mine, David Barksby. We enlisted at Derby and then went on to Carlisle for training. It seemed like a good idea at the time. I was young and single, and felt like trying something different, and there was no-one to stop me going. My father had died in 1956, a year after I left school, so I was the breadwinner now. And he'd had twenty-one years in the Army himself, so he would probably have approved. The only trouble was, I soon found out I didn't like it. David stayed and made a career of it, but after a couple of months I couldn't take any more and bought myself out. When I think about it now, I reckon it was the strict discipline that did it for me. I'd had plenty of that with my father while I was growing up, and that was fair enough, but being shouted at and bullied day in day out was more than I could stand. After I came out I had three years with a chrome-plating firm at the Sheepbridge Works on the north side of

Chesterfield, then I came back to the job I'd wanted when I first left school, working down Arkwright pit.

At Arkwright I was back on the 'materials' with the mechanical hauler like I'd been at Markham No 1. Here, though, the colliery didn't have shafts like Markham. An automated man-hauler ran cars on rails, carrying sixty or seventy men at a time on a four hundred metre journey down to the pit bottom, then off to different underground districts to work. When I'd first applied for a job at Arkwright, there had been maybe three hundred men working there. By the time I finished in 1986 it was closer to a thousand; as other pits in the area closed down, men were redirected to Arkwright and to Markham for work. Once underground, the atmosphere was cold and wet, and the pumps worked overtime to keep the level of water down. Some of it was pumped above ground to be purified, and then reused on the machines at the coal-face. I did six years at the face as a ripper, and fitting chocks to shore up the roof (Figure 8). The

Figure 8. Night shift, Arkwright Colliery, 10 pm, in 1983. Waiting to go underground are (left to right) Jimmy Fishwick, Jack Rayner, Jimmy Cutts, Harold Bennett and Charles Dickens. *Author's collection*

Figure 9. The Station Hotel. *Edwin Rotherham Collection*

ripping machine would move up and down the face, shearing off the coal with a set of picks. These were changed on a regular basis by a fitter who was always on hand to ensure they didn't get too blunted by the work. There was a fair amount of dust about, but thanks to the water sprayed through the machinery it didn't become unbearable. And the money was always good for face work.

By the time I was in my teens I'd started to get interested in things other than football, like most lads of my age. Several of us used to go to the dances they had every Saturday night at the upstairs room in the *Station Hotel* (Figure 9), and meet up with the girls. They didn't have live bands there then, it was dancing to records, but I know I enjoyed my evenings there. There were girls at the Youth Club, too. Several of my friends married Arkwright girls, but I met one from Hady. Her name was Maureen Clark. We first met at the *Somerset House* pub in Calow, where I used to go drinking with some of my pals, and we soon got to know each other and began courting. When we got married in 1963 I moved away from Arkwright, and although I often went back to visit my friends, I never returned there to live. My mother, who hadn't been well for years, died in 1978.

I was out of Arkwright when all the big changes took place. In 1988, not long after Arkwright Colliery closed, they found that methane gas was leaking into some of the houses. They installed some kind of meter to keep an eye on it, but it scared a lot of the people there. Then in 1993 British Coal came up with the idea of opencasting a massive site on both sides of the road (Figure 10). To do it, they had to knock down the old village and build a new one across the road and a bit further down. I can only think it must have been worth their while, because moving Arkwright must have cost no end of money. By 1996 the last houses of the old village had been

Figure 10. Bulldozers on the Arkwright opencast site. *Edwin Rotherham Collection*

Figure 11. A view of the new Arkwright Town, on the opposite side of the road. *Dennis Middleton*

demolished, and the new Arkwright was up and running (Figure 11). Apart from Mr Perrins' house, nothing was left of the place I'd known as a boy (Figure 12).

I've been back plenty of times since then, and I hear different

Figure 12. Mr Perrins' house, Chesterfield Road. *Dennis Middleton*

stories. Some think it's great in the new village, but others miss the comradeship and neighbourliness that the old Arkwright used to have. They'd like to be back there, but there's no way that can happen, is there?

It's all gone now, and in the past. But I know that I lived at a wonderful time, in the best village in the world. There were 152 houses in Arkwright, and I've been in every one and been made welcome there. And though it's gone, I'll always have my memories.

Acknowledgements

I would like to thank my good friend Mr Edwin Rotherham for his help with some of my early recollections, and for the loan of several photographs from his private collection.

Notes & References

1. Kelly & Co Ltd, *Directory of Derbyshire*, 1899, p 366.

6. GHOSTS OF CHESTERFIELD

by Carol Brindle

ONE SUNDAY EVENING, not far into the reign of Queen Victoria, people living in the huddled buildings in the Shambles heard 'murderous noises'[1] coming from behind the door of a butcher's shop. Jack Platts, then minding the business, was known to be a bit of a rogue and many immediately feared for his girlfriend, Hannah. But someone knew that she was in church. Jack's voice called out and assured them that all was well, and so the neighbours went back home. If they had been more persistent they may well have prevented a tragedy (Figure 1).

In September of the following year, two night-soil workers arrived at Falcon Yard opposite the Shambles, to empty the cesspit jointly owned by Mr Bunting, a corn dealer, and the grocer Mr Towndrow

Figure 1. The Shambles, scene of the Collis murder in 1845. *Dennis Middleton*

Figure 2. Falcon Yard, where the body of George Collis was found buried in a cess pit. *Dennis Middleton*

(Figure 2). To the horror of the workers, Robert Ashley and Valentine Wall, the contents of the cesspit also revealed mangled human remains including a skull which had been fractured. The owners of the privies were summoned together with Dr Walker and they identified the remains as a dismembered human body and not the sheep carcass the night-soil workers had originally thought it to be. The presence of clothing in the pit gave final, grim confirmation. A good black coat, canary-coloured waistcoat, black silk neckerchief with the initials G C, trousers with braces still attached, and a single garter. Last of all a hat, bearing damage which corresponded with the state of the skull. The clothing helped to identify the corpse as that of George Collis, a young man of twenty-five who had worked at Hasland House until the death of the owner, when he had gone to work for the butcher, Jack Platts. His girlfriend, Ellen Beresford, had the other garter.

A coroner's inquest met at the *Shoulder of Mutton* inn at Hasland, and according to the unfortunately worded report 'sat on the remains'[2] from 10 am until 7.30 pm. They agreed that a foul murder had been committed and those people living in the Shambles, who had themselves described the 'murderous noises', were rebuked for not alerting the authorities. Ellen Beresford identified what was left of her lover's body, and produced the matching garter as further confirmatory evidence.

That fateful Sunday night George had visited Ellen, who was pregnant by him, and given her the garter as a keepsake. He told her that he intended to visit the butcher's shop to get money which Jack Platts owed him. He had given his savings to be in partnership with Platts who was not 'over scrupulous'[3] in dealing honestly with the naïve young man. Once he had received the money, George said he meant to go to Manchester with a friend to look for work and he also expressed fears that he might be murdered. He consulted his watch before he parted from Ellen. Furthermore, he told his mother of his plans to go to Manchester, and informed her he 'should not write'.[4]

So the absence of George Collis between that Sunday evening in December 1845, and the later Sunday evening of September 1846 was not remarked on because everyone thought he was in Manchester, when in fact he was much closer to home.

George's watch was found in the possession of Jack Platts' mother, who had redeemed it after it had been pawned by Platts himself. Mr Thompson the watchmaker had taken note of the number when he sold it to George, so there was no doubting its identity. Platts claimed he bought it from 'Lanky Bill', but 'Lanky' promptly denied this.

Jack Platts was arrested for the wilful murder of George Collis. He was taken to Derby Gaol, where he was tried and sentenced to death. He was hanged there on 1 April 1847. His request that he be executed in the morning to avoid crowds coming from Chesterfield to witness the event was denied. Public hangings were a popular spectator sport in the early nineteenth century, and many travelled from Platts' home town to see him die, still protesting his innocence, for the murder of George Collis.

George's ghost is said to haunt the Shambles, perhaps trying to shame all those who might have prevented his murder that night. He was down the privy for ten months, so it seems likely that any would-be ghost hunters will smell him before they see him!

Although the new Woolworth store is now located on Vicar Lane, its predecessor stood for many years at the end of Burlington Street not far from the parish church. Many workers at the stores, and customers too, were disturbed by the 'strange feeling' at the rear of the shopfloor. Women told of never going into a store room area alone because of the 'cold and eerie' atmosphere. One lady tells of being sent to weigh out nails in a store room and feeling them to be hot. Most disturbing of all, many spoke of hearing screaming and crying and smelt smoke, even though there was no fire in the vicinity. Few had heard of the terrible fire which occurred on 27 December 1911 in that very place.

Before the Woolworth stores were built, the site was occupied by the Palace cinema, popularly known as the Picture Palace. At that time the film industry was in its infancy and the reels very short, not long enough to occupy an entire evening. To increase the length of the entertainment, dancing shows were arranged using the talent of local girls in their early teens or younger. In fact, Lizzie Bell was only twelve years old and very excited at appearing for the first time in a show, having had permission from Robinson's, her employers, to take the afternoon off. About thirty young girls gathered in a room in an adjacent building owned by the Palace management, which was heated by an open fire. By some awful mischance Lizzie's highly flammable Eskimo costume caught fire. Panic-stricken, she rushed around with the flames setting other costumes alight before she fled from the building. Her agonised screams alerted people waiting at the side entrance for the show to begin, who quickly put out the flames. Lizzie's father, Fred Bell, lived in nearby Roberts' Yard, and came running when he heard the commotion. Finding a child with fire-blackened face and burnt clothing, he asked her name. It was Lizzie. So badly disfigured was she, Fred had failed to recognise his own daughter. 'Take me to Mummy', she begged.[5]

In the panic that ensued many children were burned or trampled. The staff at the hospital were alerted and the injured girls were rushed there together with adults who had suffered injury trying to save them. Five little girls died of burns, among them Lizzie Bell and her friend Ada, who had tried to help by beating at the flames on Lizzie's costume with her hands, until her own clothing caught fire. The funerals took place on 1 January 1912 and the girls were buried in Spital churchyard.

Is it any wonder that echoes of this terrible event still linger on this

Figure 3. The Burger King restaurant, Burlington Street, site of the 'Picture Palace' fire of 1911. *Dennis Middleton*

site such as screams and cries and the smell of smoke? (Figure 3)

In the mid-1970s the cellar of the Woolworth store was re-concreted. A workman left his tools neatly lined up and locked the door behind him. Next day his tools were in disarray, and there was a single footprint in the concrete.

It is not recorded what size the footprint was.

The Old Registry on Newbold Road has had many functions over the past hundred years. During the time it was the Social Services offices strange events occurred. A man who was known to work late on many occasions suddenly changed his working hours to avoid staying later than 7 pm. Apparently one night when working late he heard the door open, and footsteps followed by the sound of buckets and mopping. Believing it to be the cleaners, he turned to greet them, only to find he was completely alone. Nothing would make him work late in that office again.

One of a team of cleaners working in the same building saw what she took to be a new colleague cleaning in an office. She noticed that this lady's clothes were rather old-fashioned, but thought little of it. After all, who wears new clothes when cleaning? When the shift was finished, she asked her supervisor if she should fetch the new lady, as she could not have left the building without passing them. The supervisor knew nothing about a new team member. Was it the phantom cleaner heard by the man working late in that same office? There seems to be no explanation for this phenomenon. Is Chesterfield unique in having a building haunted by ghostly cleaners? The awful thought arises that a lack of attention to housework in this world may result in the punishment of having to clean for eternity. A truly dreadful prospect!

A woman cleaning at Tapton House when it was a school had a strange experience. She was sweeping the steps in a corridor at the end of which were stone steps leading to a locked door. Looking up from her work, she saw before her a gentleman in Victorian dress demanding to know why she had not brought up his hot water that morning! The cleaner was shocked into silence, so he repeated the question. The woman eventually found her voice but was so frightened that she apologised, even though she was not the servant this apparition evidently mistook her for. On being shown pictures by the headmaster she immediately identified the man as the railway pioneer George Stephenson, who had lived in the house for the ten years up to his death in 1848. She had never seen a picture of him before.

A young schoolgirl, who visited Tapton House at a time when it was disused, did not know what George Stephenson looked like either, although she knew he was buried at Holy Trinity Church on Newbold Road in the town itself. She had declined a dare to explore the deserted Tapton House with her schoolfriends, but returned later on her own. Thrilled at finding an old carriage in the coach house she climbed aboard and imagined what it must have been like to be a lady travelling in such a fine vehicle. Sensing that she was being watched, she looked up to see a gentleman studying her from nearby. He wore a tall hat and thick side-whiskers not fashionable at the time. Although this man said nothing, merely smiling at her in a kindly way, the girl had the compelling feeling that she should not be there, and at once ran all the way home.

The state of her clothing – for the carriage had been very dusty –

and her agitated manner alerted her parents, and the girl finally confessed to what she had seen. Her father, who had been a footman at Tapton House when the Markham family lived there, immediately recognised her description as that of Mr Stephenson himself. He explained that George was often seen wandering around the house, which he had loved so much during his life.

The Memorial Hall built in memory of George Stephenson is now the home of the Pomegranate (formerly the Civic) Theatre (Figure 4). The ghostly presence there is referred to as 'George' and a figure in clothing resembling that of the Victorian era has been seen, but mostly the haunting takes the form of footsteps, doors banging open of their own accord, and a smell of tobacco smoke. The last is thought to indicate the spirit of an actor who often worked at the theatre. An amateur drama group, enjoying refreshments in a room

Figure 4. Stephenson Memorial Hall and Pomegranate Theatre, Corporation Street, favourite visiting places for the ghost of railway pioneer George Stephenson. *Dennis Middleton*

Figure 5. The Yorkshire Bank, formerly Old Manor House, scene of ghostly emanations. *Dennis Middleton*

in the Pomegranate, were astounded when they heard a perfectly normal piano begin to play all by itself!

There was once another theatre down Corporation Street, the Hippodrome. In 1925 a group of professional actors was engaged to perform the pantomime 'Rip Van Winkle'. A local girl, who had been auditioned successfully as a dancer, went along to the stage door to attend rehearsals after school. Since no one else joined her she went through the stage door alone and found herself in a dark corridor. She was quite concerned but reassured when she felt an arm around her shoulder, guiding her towards what proved to be a door leading on to the stage. She turned to express her gratitude to her helper, only to find no-one there. The actors onstage were also amazed to see her talking to thin air, as it seemed to them. When she told them her story, they showed her a room which many people had refused to enter, as an actor had once died there. Could that long dead thespian have been helping a young hopeful to her stage debut, perhaps?

Often there seems to be no explanation for ghostly appearances, or the stories which might explain them have been forgotten and lost. This is the case with the Yorkshire Bank, an impressive building that once bore the title The Old Manor House (Figure 5). At least three women saw strange apparitions there. One, waiting in the dining room for her husband, heard strange clanking noises and was joined by a ghost complete with chain. With great presence of mind she fled from the room and locked the door behind her, but the spectre merely clanked through the closed door and back into the hall. The woman's sister also saw something which she recalled as horrible beyond description. As she was holding a Bible at the time she threw the book at the spirit, which promptly disappeared. On a subsequent occasion, another female relative saw a baby on the floor upstairs. Puzzled, she bent to pick it up, only to find her arms plunging straight through the tiny body. Her flight down the stairs involved only small landings and not the seven steps in between each one! People working in the bank have described strange happenings in our own day, including a computer terminal in the former dining room which unlike all the other machines was forever going wrong and breaking down. Cleaners describe queue dividers which moved even though no-one touched them and there was not so much as a draught to blow them. Telephones rang round the building at night despite having been switched down to operate only through the Night Supervisor's own handset.

The reasons for these phenomena may never be known, but legend has it that the murder of a coachman at the nearby *Sun Inn* is to blame for the strange events there. The former *Sun Inn*, etched three times on the windows of the present building, was a coaching house with a stable yard, and had a cellar with a deep well (Figure 6). It is said that

Figure 6. The *Sun Inn*, West Bars, last resting place of the murdered coachman. *Dennis Middleton*

Figure 7. The Town Hall, Rose Hill, once the location of Rose Hill House and its ghostly bells. *Dennis Middleton*

the coachman's body was pushed down into the well and that his unquiet spirit is responsible for the many eerie happenings in the cellar, which survives from the original building. Footsteps have been heard padding around the now much reduced well opening. In the 1950s the publican was alerted by noises in the locked cellar and found that empty bottle cases were scattered across the floor. He re-stacked them, only to hear more noises and find the cases again in disarray. The family's Alsatian dog refused point-blank to enter the cellar, as did any other dogs who were brought to the inn. Whatever spirit was disturbing them must have been strong, as the stiff taps on the barrels in the cellar had also been switched off, preventing beer from reaching the bar pumps! Another publican found that the coolers had been switched off. All of these events took place behind locked doors.

The present Town Hall was once the location of a three-storey private residence called Rose Hill House, which stood in its own nine acres of ground (Figure 7). In 1830, when the house was roughly a century old, a Mr Ashwell moved in. After some time, he and his family encountered problems with the bells that were rung to summon the servants. These bells began to ring unaided, without anyone having operated the bell pull. There was no predicting this unscheduled ringing; sometimes months passed uneventfully, but sooner or later the ghostly ringing returned. Fearing some prank, Mr Ashwell is said to have locked his servants in the library to ensure they were not involved. Finding that the bells rang on regardless, he set about trying to solve the puzzle. One bell always rang first even when its position was changed, and the bells rang in a regular pendulum arc until they suddenly stopped. In desperation Mr Ashwell had the bells disconnected by cutting the wires, but they rang once again. A workman called in to reconnect them was horrified when a bell rang in his face before he had begun to fix it back to its wire! He slid rapidly down his ladder, left tools and ladder behind, and ran.

The old Royal Hospital on Holywell Cross is a fine, imposing structure, but many people have reported the eerie atmosphere in Nightingale Ward, the children's ward. It is claimed that a nurse committed suicide there following the death of a child due to a wrongly administered dose of oxygen. Nurses tell of the problems they often had with the oxygen cylinders, which appeared to have been tampered with. It became so worrying that a porter was assigned to sit and watch the cylinders. This proved a restful task for him, until a spanner – used to adjust the valves altering the flow of the gas – rose from a table of its own volition and moved towards a cylinder. The terrified porter fled from the room. It is to be hoped he was not the same porter who one night entered the mortuary to find a ghostly figure sitting on a trolley there!

One nurse remembers being on night duty and instructed to keep an eye on a terminally ill patient, who was not expected to last the night. Seeing a man in naval uniform seated by the bed, she assumed he was a visitor who had been allowed to sit by the dying man. It did occur to her that the uniform was rather old-fashioned, with epaulettes and gold tassels. The supposed visitor was seen at the end of the ward, smiling sadly. Before the nurse could ask him who he was, he melted away. Was he a long dead relative, come to accompany the dying man on his last journey?

Behind the black and white timbered buildings on Knifesmithgate stands the late seventeenth century Unitarian chapel in Elder Yard. The chapel's graveyard had to be cleared for the buildings, and some claim that although the gravestones were moved, not all the graves were emptied. Could this account for all the unusual events in the buildings which now form part of the Victoria Centre? (Figures 8 & 9)

Figure 8. View along Knifesmithgate, leading to Victoria Centre. *Dennis Middleton*

Figure 9. Victoria Centre, Knifesmithgate, scene of the ropewalk ghost. *Dennis Middleton*

Originally a cinema stood here, and after it was closed, its old projection room was used for storage. Many people commented on the unpleasant atmosphere in this area, and described their feelings of terror. Some of them were shocked when a young man who had been sent to count work-tops in the projection room ran down to the shop floor, evidently distraught. When he calmed down he told of having felt a drop in the temperature, and then the terrifying sensation of arms encircling him. As they gripped him tighter, they seemed to grow hotter and hotter. With the strength of sheer terror, he managed to break free. He never worked in that room again.

It was later discovered that the Victoria Brass Foundry, owned by the Oliver family, once occupied the site. Apprentices were often warned about the danger of becoming entangled in ropes that were attached to pulleys for lifting heavy castings. One unfortunate young man did become ensnared in this way, and the ropes, counterbalanced by the weight on the other end, hauled him up to the roof. When his lifeless body was retrieved, it was horribly apparent that the ropes had crushed and compressed his waist, causing death by suffocation. He must have felt like that frightened young man in the projection room years later, as if arms were gripping him, burning hotter and hotter as their terrible grip grew ever tighter... .

Perhaps such terror lasts beyond death itself?

Notes and References

1. *Derby Mercury*, 9 September 1846 p.3 c.4, report of inquest held 3 September 1846.
2. *Ibid.*
3. *Derby Mercury*, 16 September 1846 p.4, report of second inquest held 10 September 1846.
4. *Derby Mercury*, 9 September 1846 p.3 c.4.
5. *Derbyshire Times*, 30 December 1911.

7. VICTORIAN WINGERWORTH – A 'CLOSE' PARISH?

by David G Edwards

Introduction

RURAL PARISHES ARE SOMETIMES CLASSIFIED historically into 'close' and 'open' kinds, depending on whether incomers found it difficult or easy respectively to obtain a 'settlement' in the place, making the parish liable to maintain them if they fell on hard times. Close parishes were generally those where one or two major landowners monopolised the freehold and were thus able to control society there, restricting the influx of outsiders and hence the number of paupers chargeable on the rates.[1]

The Hunloke family owned some 2,700 of the 2,900 acres of Wingerworth in 1843[2] and appear to have done so since at least the early eighteenth century,[3] so theoretically at least the parish was a 'close' one. Although by the time of Queen Victoria's accession in 1837 the distinction between close and open parishes had become blurred, especially as a result of the reformation of the Poor Law in 1834 and gradual industrialisation, the idea still forms a useful background to a consideration of the nature of Wingerworth society between about 1840 and 1900. I discussed the question more generally several years ago,[4] but my subsequent analysis of further sources now allows me, I hope, to draw more particular and better conclusions for the Victorian period.

Wingerworth parish records provide an illustration, albeit from earlier in the nineteenth century, of a concern to prevent casual workers from gaining a settlement certificate by residence for a full year in the parish. These records include two volumes of standard forms of agreement by which servants bound themselves to farmers and other employers for periods of no more than fifty-one weeks at a time.[5] Many of these servants were doubtless engaged at the Chesterfield or Ashover hiring fairs. For instance, John Gratton jnr of Lydgate Farm employed Bathia Fretwell for fifty-one weeks from 21 November 1818 and then immediately again, by a new agreement, for another fifty-one weeks from 15 November 1819. From 1834, poor relief was no longer the responsibility of the individual parish, so this particular concern disappeared. Wingerworth's expenditure on the poor in the early nineteenth century was in fact very moderate, averaging £165 per year.[6]

Population

The Hunlokes of Wingerworth Hall, as well as the Gladwins of Stubbing Court with their much smaller estate, were able to restrict the number of houses built in the parish and hence limit the population to that necessary to work the land and provide essential services. It was actually recorded that in the 1840s Sir Henry Hunloke did not wish any more houses to be built in Wingerworth.[7] Thus the population of Wingerworth remained well below 500 throughout the Victorian era, even declining, as Table 1 shows, in contrast to nearby Tupton and Clay Cross.

Table 1. Wingerworth population compared with Tupton and Clay Cross

Year	Wingerworth	Tupton	Clay Cross
1841	482 (89)*	317	1478
1851	463 (93)	270	2278
1861	433 (88)	1004	4096
1871	385 (81)	1062	5140
1881	410 (81)	1374	6347
1891	379 (76)	1551	7138
1901	387 (79)**	1796	7445

* Figures in parentheses are numbers of households; the figures for 1841 are corrected for one duplicated entry in the census return.
** Omitting the 'household' of two men sleeping in a barn on census night.

The Hunloke 'interregnum' between the deaths of the last two baronets without issue in 1856 and the succession to the estate in 1864 of a cousin[8] seems to have been marked by some 'improvements' which included demolition of poorer cottages in Wingerworth without the erection of an equal number of new houses. Other properties were demolished both before and after that period, making a total of eighteen between 1841 and 1901, some of which had housed more than one family, whereas apart from replacements of three existing properties only eight new houses appeared, three of which were not on the Hunloke estate. The numbers of households recorded in the censuses are seen in Table 1.

It might be thought that in a 'close' parish one would largely find the same families residing for generation upon generation, and in the same houses, but this would hardly have been true of parishes in which householders had only annual or even monthly tenancies, as in Wingerworth.[9] Only for a few Wingerworth properties can the same family be recognised in residence for more than one or two generations in the period for which complete lists of Hunloke tenants are available (early eighteenth to early twentieth century). One of those few families was the Watsons, three generations of whom lived successively at Pear Tree Farm (on the lane named after them) from the 1770s to the 1860s.[10]

The census returns show that of the fifty-six houses in the parish (other than the Hall and Stubbing Court) that existed continuously from 1841 to 1901, only four were inhabited by the same family over the whole period: Rock House at Stone Edge (Dronfield family), Pond House at Stubbing (Swift), Bay Tree Farm on Bole Hill (Mellor) and Belfit Hill Farm (Goodlad). Another six were occupied by the same family at six successive censuses, and another four by the same family at five in succession. In contrast, Lydgate Farm (generally the largest in Wingerworth) had a different tenant family at each census from 1841 to 1881: Gratton in 1841 was followed by Lowe in 1851, Potter in 1861, Hadfield in 1871 and Fisher in 1881-1901; moreover, other sources show yet more changes there, with tenants Leason in 1855, Lee in 1857 and Revell in 1864.[11] Reasons for the fairly frequent changes in tenancy in Wingerworth may only be guessed at. Death is an obvious one; others may well have included bad behaviour, bankruptcy, or simply a wish to move to a better situation elsewhere.

In this connection, we can also look at the birthplaces of the household heads as shown by the census returns. Table 2 shows that, far from being a parish full of native-born tenants, Wingerworth rather was a place of 'foreigners', becoming more and more so up to 1881, after which the trend was reversed.

Table 2. Birthplace distribution of household heads in Wingerworth

Birthplace	**Percentage of household heads**					
	1851	**1861**	**1871**	**1881**	**1891**	**1901**
Wingerworth	39	40	26	20	24	32
Other NE Derbyshire*	36	31	35	41	31	33
Derbyshire elsewhere	13	12	16	15	12	6
Yorks/Notts/Staffs	5	10	11	11	16	10
Elsewhere	7	7	12	14	17	18

* Parishes in the present Chesterfield, Bolsover and North East Derbyshire local authority districts, plus the former North Derbyshire parishes now in Sheffield.

A similar picture emerges from the birthplaces of the wives of the household heads. A particular influx of outsiders seems to have occurred in the 1860s, for which the new Hunloke owners were no doubt partly responsible: Adelaide and Frederick Hunloke had come to Wingerworth from the London area and, having partly aristocratic origins, were no doubt anxious to secure the most desirable class of tenant and estate servant from outside the parish. One example is perhaps the carpenter Edwin Hardy, a native of Wiltshire who arrived in the 1860s.

Of course, the outsiders did not necessarily move to Wingerworth directly from their places of birth. Earlier movements of some of them can be traced from the birthplaces of their children recorded in the census returns. William Froggatt, for instance, who was the Hunlokes' head gardener for nearly forty years, was born in Barlborough in 1812 but appears to have come to Wingerworth about 1849 from the East Riding, where his first six children were born (the eldest at Hotham, the others at nearby Market Weighton; his wife's birthplace was Aston, Staffs.). He had perhaps worked on the Hotham Hall estate. James Butler, the first resident land agent employed by Adelaide Hunloke, was born in the village of Britford in Wiltshire about 1820, but the three of his sons living with him in 1871 had been born in Chilton Foliat in the same county, so he may have been previously employed at Chilton House; his wife was a native of Berkshire.

Occasionally someone born in Wingerworth returning to his native parish can be discerned. One such was George Alexander Clay, born illegitimately in 1810 and put out as a parish apprentice in 1819 with stone merchant Jesse Rutherford of Bole Hill Farm,[12] who evidently trained him as a stonecutter, in which capacity he returned to Wingerworth in the 1850s with his wife (a native of Sutton Bonington, Notts.) and three young children who were born at Heage.

The converse of the above, the emigration of Wingerworth-born people, can be detected from the census returns for other places. Examination of the 1851 returns for Chesterfield borough, Walton, Clay Lane, Woodthorpe, Tupton, North Wingfield, Temple Normanton, Hasland and Ashover, revealed 123 persons in those nearby townships who had been born in Wingerworth, of which 34 were heads of household. In Chesterfield they included a thirteen-year-old boy in the Workhouse, and in Walton the John Gratton who in 1841 had been at Lydgate Farm in Wingerworth. Often the 'foreigners' too did not remain in the parish for long.

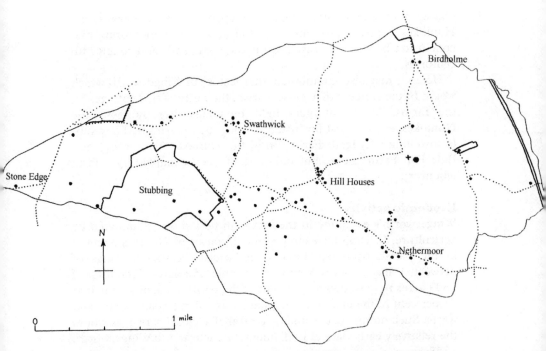

Figure 1. Hunloke land and sites of houses in Wingerworth in 1843, as revealed by the tithe survey. Sir Henry Hunloke owned the whole of the parish except those areas outlined in bold, i.e. the Stubbing Court estates, church lands and the North Midland Railway. Wingerworth Hall is shown as the bold dot nearest the church. Dotted lines are roads.

Settlement pattern

Figure 1 shows how much of the parish was owned by the Hunlokes in 1843, and the sites of the houses then, as revealed by the tithe commutation survey.[2] As can be seen, there was no large group of houses at any site: nothing that could really be called a village. What appears to have been the last of a true village of Wingerworth (a group of eight houses on the hill south of the Hall) was swept away around 1800;[13] this was evidently the Hunlokes' final step in making their residence as private as possible. The scattered settlement that became a feature of the parish may have been due partly to a 'divide and rule' policy on the part of the Hunlokes. However, Wingerworth had never had a completely consolidated village, except perhaps in Anglo-Saxon and Norman times: for example, in the west of the parish, Swathwick and Stubbing had become settled in the medieval period. In itself, scattered settlement might suggest an 'open' parish, but because the Hunlokes controlled so much of the area, we cannot draw that conclusion here, or at least not for the eighteenth and nineteenth centuries.

Here we may also mention another feature of Wingerworth which would fit the concept of a 'close' parish: the rarity of tied cottages on the farms. Most cottagers held tenancies directly from the Hunlokes, and in 1864 for instance,[14] only three farms had any sub-let dwellings: Lydgate Farm (one), the Hunloke Arms (one) and Bole Hill Farm (three, but only one of them occupied by a farm labourer).

Economic activity

Wingerworth's economy in the Victorian period was dominated by agriculture. In 1843 for example, the 23 farms of 20 acres or more in the parish occupied 1557 acres, whilst 31 smallholdings of between 1 and 20 acres occupied a further 252 acres.[2] The total of 1809 acres represented 62 per cent of the parish area, or as much as 85 per cent of the area not occupied by woodland, roads, water and waste. Such dominance would be typical of a 'close' parish, as would the relatively early date of parliamentary enclosure in Wingerworth, 1758.

Besides farming, other economic activities were also important, even if none of them actually employed more than a few Wingerworth residents. Forestry is perhaps the most obvious of these, since over 700 acres of Wingerworth was occupied by woods at that time. Many of these woods were cultivated by felling small and large timber, with replacement by replanting or allowing re-growth of coppiced trees. One particular wood sale, on 21 December 1864, brought in over £1,000 for the Hunlokes.[15] A few Wingerworth residents (William Goodlad and John Mellor in 1851, Henry Handbury in 1901) were recorded as timber merchants, but no more than five manual forestry workers (sawyers etc.) were noted at any of the censuses from 1841 to 1901. Additional workers were presumably brought in from neighbouring districts as need be, and this would not have been surprising, given that the Hunlokes owned considerable property in nearby parishes.

Another important product was stone, quarried at two main sites, Bole Hill and Stone Edge, and worked up at a sawmill on Pearce Lane; ganister was extracted in Ivy Spring Wood.[16] Again, few quarry workers are recorded in the Wingerworth census returns, and here too, extra men were presumably employed from elsewhere. The Rutherfords of Bole Hill Farm (Jesse and then his son William) operated both main quarries up to mid Victorian times; subsequently the Margeresons took over at Bole Hill, followed by Booth Waddington, whereas Stone Edge quarry was eventually acquired by Percy Turner of Grindleford. James Pearson, Whittington Moor pottery manufacturer, seems to have operated the ganister quarry in the 1860s[17] and may have brought in his own workers.

A further important industry in Wingerworth was of course coal mining. Bell-pits and other small collieries had been sunk since early times, and the western outcrops had become practically exhausted, e.g. that of the Blackshale in Speighthill Wood. Larger-scale operations were begun in the Victorian period in two areas: between Speighthill Wood and Longedge Lane, and east of Derby Road near the River Rother. These took place under mineral leases granted by the Hunlokes, who were evidently not entirely averse to despoliation of the landscape as long as it earned them income. The former area was exploited by Wingerworth Iron Company, whose ironworks were not in the parish but on Storforth Lane (at that time in Hasland); mining began in the 1840s but appears to have ceased well before 1900; output is said to have been *c*.400 tons per day.[18] The latter area was developed by Wingerworth Coal Company, which sank Old Avenue Pit (depth only 235 ft) in 1857, and subsequently by Clay Cross Company, which sank Avenue Colliery (Clay Cross No.9, depth 765 ft) in 1881. Old Avenue Colliery was abandoned in the 1880s, but Avenue continued working until about 1930 and employed several hundred workers. Nearly all of those obviously lived outside Wingerworth, although more colliery employees (as many as twenty-five, exceptionally, in 1901) than forestry or quarry workers were recorded in the Wingerworth census returns.

As well as coal, Wingerworth Iron Co. mined ironstone in the Speighthill area until the 1870s, when the seams became exhausted; output has been reported as 2,000 tons per week. Again only very few iron miners are recorded in the Wingerworth census returns. One small piece of evidence, if one were needed, for outside employees is a report[19] of serious injuries from a rock fall in one of the Speighthill ironstone pits in 1856: the victim was a labourer from Brampton, indicating that workers were prepared to travel some distance to work in Wingerworth.

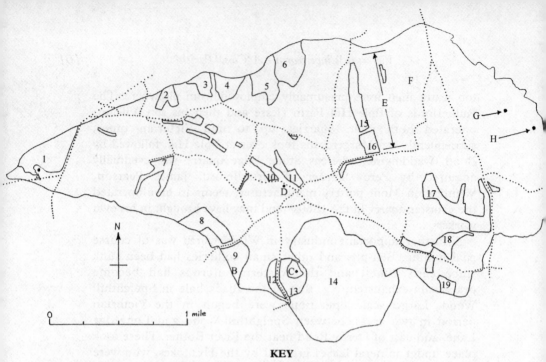

1. Stone Edge Plantation; 2. Clayton Wood; 3. Wellspring Wood; 4. Robin Croft and Windsor Woods; 5. Emmetfield and Cowley Upper Woods; 6. Widdowson Spring Wood; 7. Gladwin Wood; 8. Cowley Wood; 9. Ivy Spring Wood; 10. Pearce Wood; 11. Bradbury Wood; 12. Bole Hill Woods; 13. Red Carr Plantation; 14. Hardwick Wood; 15/16. Nether and Upper Speighthill Woods; 17. Hanging Banks Plantation; 18. Sutcliffe Wood; 19. Button Hill Plantation; A. Stone Edge Quarry; B. Gannister quarry; C. Bole Hill Quarry; D. Stone sawmill; E. Area of iron stone mining; F. Speighthill Colliery; G. Avenue Colliery; H. Old Avenue Colliery.

Figure 2. Main areas of woodland in Wingerworth in 1843, as revealed by the tithe survey, and main sites of industry in Victorian times. *Wingerworth tithe map and award 1843, D2360/3/34b, 34c. Derbyshire Record Office, Matlock*

Figure 2 shows the main sites of the woodland and industry in Wingerworth in our period.

Religious life

It may be supposed that in many 'close' parishes, religious life was completely dominated by the Anglican church. However, Wingerworth does not fit that picture entirely. In the first place, Wingerworth was not a fully fledged ecclesiastical parish until 1867, merely a chapelry in Chesterfield parish (although for a long time its church had had a degree of independence), and until elevated to rector that year its incumbent was only a perpetual curate, receiving only a fraction of the tithes, though owning some glebe. Moreover, in mid-century, services appear to have been held only once each Sunday (morning and afternoon alternately).[20] Second, there had long been a Roman Catholic influence, even a following, in Wingerworth due to the Hunlokes' religious faith and the activities of their private priests.[21] Third, there had also been some Dissenters in the parish from time to time and applications were made in 1826 and 1840 to register houses as meeting-places for Nonconformist worship.[22]

All this suggests that Anglican control over Wingerworth's inhabitants was in practice quite lax at the time. This was proved when, in the mid-1840s, Joseph Fletcher obtained a supervisory post in the Wingerworth Iron Co.'s mines and began evangelising in the parish. According to his own account,[7] he found a ready audience among the ordinary folk, so much so that he was ready to build his own chapel in Wingerworth. Here he was up against opposition not only from the curate, Reverend Samuel Revel, but also from Sir Henry Hunloke. This meant that no Hunloke land (and no Gladwin land either, apparently, and certainly no church land!) was available for a chapel. It was therefore fortunate for Fletcher that a small independent area of freehold still existed in Wingerworth, in the hands of the Grattons at Stubbing, which he indeed managed to purchase and where he built Salem chapel in 1849.[2, 23]

Conclusion
The picture of Victorian Wingerworth that emerges, therefore, is of a parish with two major landowners who between them controlled practically the whole area, exercised social control and restricted (even reduced) housing development and population growth, but where there was much turnover of the population, industrial activity needing appreciable numbers of day workers from outside, uncertain religious control, and still a small amount of land available for independent use. In addition, the concept of a parish boundary was blurred by the fact that the lands of the Hunlokes and the Gladwins ran over into adjacent parishes.

We conclude from this that although Wingerworth might seem to have satisfied the criteria for a 'close' parish in some respects, in others it was very 'leaky', and could not be considered a closed community. Thus, as hinted at the beginning of this article, the strict distinction between close and open is only an ideal concept, useful perhaps as a starting-point but often breaking down when parishes are examined in more detail. Wingerworth was certainly not entirely 'close' in Victorian times, even if the notion can be considered at all valid for such a late period.

Notes and References

1. J Richardson, *The Local Historian's Encyclopedia*, 1974, entries B14, B53; see also for example G Ewart Evans, *Where Beards Wag All*, 1970, ch. 11.

2. Derbyshire Record Office, D2360/3/34b, 34c (*Wingerworth tithe map and award*).

3. Derbyshire Record Office, Q/RR 14/1, M6, M8 (*registers of Papists' estates: Sir Windsor and Dame Katherine Hunloke*, 1717).

4. D G Edwards, *The Hunlokes of Wingerworth Hall*, 2nd ed, 1976, 8-9.

5. Derbyshire Record Office, D2662 (*Wingerworth parish records: Service-agreement registers* 1816-33).

6. Derbyshire Record Office, 'Return from the parish of Wingerworth of the amount of the poors rate in each year ...' [1801-1817].

7. J Fletcher (ed E Nicholls), *Food for the Flock ... With an Account of the Rise and Progress of Independency at Wingerworth*, 1859, ch 2.

8. Edwards, *Hunlokes of Wingerworth Hall*, 44-6.

9. As recorded in the *Catalogue of the sale of the Hunloke estate* in 1920; cottagers were mostly on monthly tenancies then.

10. Chesterfield Local Studies Library, HUNS 1 & 2 (*terriers* of 1779 and 1819); also ref. 2 above and census returns.

11. Kelly's *Directories*, 1855 & 1864; White's *Directory*, 1857.

12. D G Edwards, *Victorian Villagers* [unpublished typescript, Chesterfield Local Studies Library], 1996, 3-5.

13. These houses are shown on a map of Wingerworth & Tupton in 1758 but not on the parish map of 1819 (Derbyshire Record Office, D1306A/PP1 & PP2 respectively).

14. Chesterfield Local Studies Library, HUNS 4 (*Terrier of the Hunloke estate*, 1864).

15. Chesterfield Local Studies Library, HUNS 5 (*Hunloke estate account book*, 1864-5).

16. E G Smith et al, *Geology of the Country around Chesterfield, Matlock and Mansfield*, 1967.

17. The account book cited above (ref. 15) includes records payment of rent by Pearson for damaged land in Ivy Spring Wood.

18. *Derbyshire Times*, 10 June 1905 (article on Wingerworth's old mines).

19. *Derbyshire Times*, 2 February 1856, 3.

20. M Tranter et al, *The Derbyshire Returns to the 1851 Religious Census*, Derbyshire Record Society, XXIII, 1995, 150

21. D G Edwards, *Hunlokes of Wingerworth Hall*, 2-3 (to which must be added that as many as seventy-five Catholics were recorded in Wingerworth in 1767: Catholic Record Society, Occasional Publication no. 2, 1989).

22. Derbyshire Record Office, Q/RR 12/110 & 119.

23. Tranter et al, *Religious Census*, 153.

8. Spital Through the Ages

by Sonia M Preece

SPITAL LIES ABOUT A MILE south-east of the parish church of All Saints, covering the area from Hady Hill to Hasland, and in its early days within viewing distance of it, before rooftops intervened. William Senior's map of 1637 shows the old crofts and roads of Chesterfield, with 'Spittle' just outside the town, east of the river, and extending to Hady Hill (Figure 1). The much later poor assessment rate map of 1826 shows Hollis Lane and Spital Lane running into an area shown as Spital Green, west of the River Rother. Spital derives its name from 'hospital', itself derived from the Latin 'hosper' (shelter by the wayside). Related names are found in Spital Lane (road or lane leading to the hospital) and Spital House (hospital house.) This article offers a view of Spital from Roman times to the present day, taking the reader along its roads and byroads, and studying a few of its many past inhabitants.

The Romans came to Chesterfield via Derby, making a camp in the fields to which the modern town owes its name (Chesterfield, from Cesterfelda, 'cester' being an Old English version of the Roman 'castra', fortified camp). The rivers Rother and Hipper provided them with a water supply, and evidence of their stay has been found at the site of the present-day *Ibis Hotel* where Hollis Lane joins the Markham Road roundabout, and at the area adjoining the church and now covered by the Vicar Lane retail development. Once the legions returned to Rome, Spital appears to have lain untouched by habitation for many years, apart from a few possibly undocumented farms, and travellers making paths from the then small town of Chesterfield, whose natives would have been numbered in scores rather than hundreds.

Leprosy was rumoured to have been brought to the area by the Knights Templar returning from the crusades, but the disease was prevalent from the eleventh through to the thirteenth century. For this two hundred year period it was a dreaded affliction for which there was no cure, and sufferers were isolated from the main community. Around 1150 the Knights Templar, who had a base at nearby Temple Normanton, founded St Leonard's Leper Hospital at the bottom of Hady Hill. St Leonard was revered by the medieval population, having a reputation as a healer, and many such hospitals

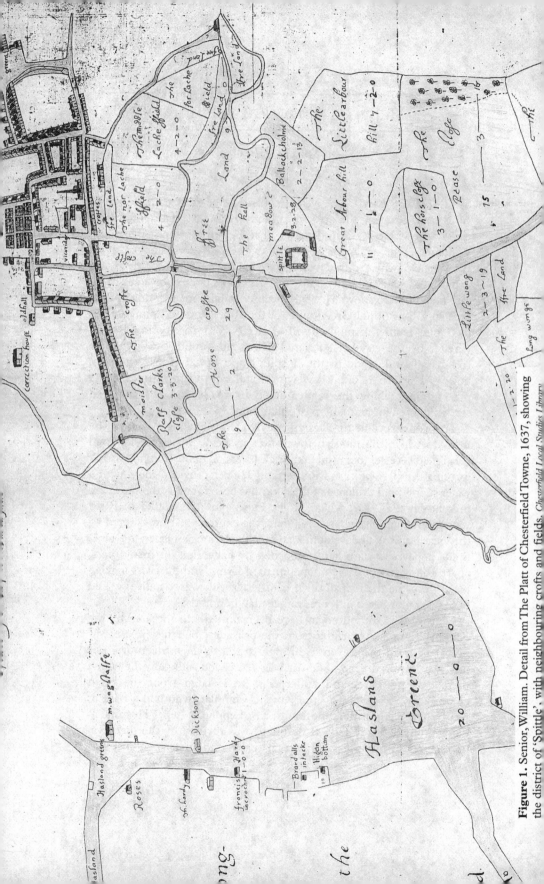

Figure 1. Senior, William. Detail from The Platt of Chesterfield Towne, 1637, showing the district of 'Spittle', with neighbouring crofts and fields. *Chesterfield Local Studies Library*

were founded in his name. The hospital was funded by fairs and markets, under the Charter of King John in 1204, which awarded it £6 per year. Lepers, cared for by the religious brethren, had a plentiful allowance of meat, fish, bread, fruit, and a gallon of ale per day, having only herbs as medicines. Other lepers not cared for in this way had to beg, warning others by the presence of their clapper and distinctive garb. They were objects of terror, to be avoided, and entering a public place was punishable by stoning.

The location of the hospital, situated on the far side of the river from the town in the belief that infection would not cross the water, was originally thought by some to be in the area of the cemetery on Hady Hill, but a recent discovery of a high status burial in one of the gardens across the road, at the junction of Picadilly Road and the main Chesterfield-Bolsover road, puts the site exactly where others presumed it to be. This burial was possibly that of one of the first monks to nurse the lepers, and is carbon dated by Sheffield University Arcus to the period 1145-1215. The bailiffs' accounts of 1474 show the annual payment of £6 to Thomas Messenger, master of St Leonard's Hospital.[1] Now, yards from his uncovering, the long-dead monk lies reburied in the grounds of Spital Cemetery by the Spital History Group, fulfilling their concern that he should be decently cared for, as he did for others (Figure 2).

Figure 2. High status medieval grave found in a garden on Picadilly Road in June 2000, dated *c.*1145-1215 and thought to be a priest at St Leonard's Leper Hospital. *Author's collection*

Figure 3. Spital House, from an old drawing. *Author's collection*

As leprosy declined, the hospital would have taken in the old and
sick to warrant the £6 per year income, but over the years it
eventually fell into decay and disappeared. From then on the fields
would have held sway, the lanes and paths being the only contact
between the hamlets.

Spital House, originally known as Spital-field House and possibly the
oldest house in Chesterfield, was built in the Elizabethan style by a Mr
Gervase Shaw in 1570, on land owned by the Earl of Shrewsbury
(husband of the redoubtable Bess of Hardwick). The occupants of
Spital House would no doubt have heard of the involvement of the
Shrewsburys with Mary Queen of Scots, their 'guest' under house arrest
at Hardwick and Chatsworth, and of her eventual execution (Figure 3).

The years of the Civil War, which divided families and property in
Chesterfield, also meant that Spital - a Royalist area - would have
suffered from the conflict. The Cavendish family, Bess's descendants,
had land confiscated by the Parliamentarians, although this was later
returned to them by Charles II. Skirmishes, one of which certainly
took place around Hady Hill, probably meant damage to buildings
and terror for the local occupants.

Spital House was occupied by a succession of eminent families. Mr Shaw was followed by the Jenkinsons in the 1640s, and a century later by the Woodyears in the 1750s, who in turn gave way to the Bourne family. In 1778 the house was home to the Mayor of Chesterfield, John Charge, who in 1837 was succeeded by a Mr Boyer. Later on, the industrialist Samuel Mason purchased the building in order to live near his substantial tobacco factory on Spital Lane.

In its issue of 1 September 1801, the *Derby Mercury* advertised the sale of plots of land in the areas of Brimington, Tapton, Calow, Spital, Hasland, Grassmoor etc. The information given with the advertisement stated:

> For the accommodation of Purchasers, the Estates are divided into a great variety of lots, several of which are very advantageously calculated for the Erection of an IRON FURNACE or other work where COAL or IRONSTONE near the spot are desirable.[2]

Evidently the industrial era had now arrived at Spital. The sale also included a cornmill, woods, and share of a manor. Anyone who tries to build on land in this area nowadays knows from experience that it was mined and used as a tipping ground, consisting mostly of shale. The advertisement continued:

> Lot No 7. A Capital Messuage or Dwelling House, with the Barns, Stables, Coach House, Outbuildings, Croft, Pleasure Grounds, and walled in gardens, pleasantly situate at Spital, near Chesterfield, late in the occupation of the Rev John Bourne, but now of Robert Jennings, Esq.[3]

The Lot, obviously Spital house itself, extended over two acres, three roods, and twelve perches. It was offered with the following fourteen lots, which included land in Hady and occupied by such locals as William Creswick, Joshua Elliott, Francis Child, and John Yates. Following the departure of its last occupant, railway manager Mr Willmott, the house was taken over by the Sisters of the Poor, in whose keeping it reverted back to a similar role as the old St Leonard's Hospital. Finally, after many years of neglect, Spital House was demolished and a new bungalow now stands on the site.

Lot No 18 was bought by Mr Herbert Mason, who built Nos 1 and 3 Alexandra Road, occupying the former with his wife Ann. No 3 was the home of his two sisters. Mr John Boyer, late of Spital House, paid £12,000 for much of the land of Spital, an area including Alexandra Road, Quarry Bank Lane, and Hartington Road.

St Leonard's, linked to the parish church of All Saints, was not the only church in Spital, others being St James' on Lordsmill Street,

Figures 4 & 5. Houses on Stanley Street, former home of Spital's factory masters. *Dennis Middleton*

and St Thomas' on Holywell Street, but religion did not always ensure a quiet life. In 1781 Benjamin Wilkinson, a follower of John Wesley, the founder of Methodism, did not receive the welcome he expected. Attempting to preach in Spital Green, he was driven out by 'the turbulence of the multitude.'[4]

Until the 1800s Spital remained mainly agricultural, but the *Enclosure Acts* of the Georgian period altered the fields from smaller plots to large fields surrounded by hedges. By the Victorian era the lace mill, tobacco factory and tannery were all thriving concerns. The census of 1841 shows James Hawley and Edwin Brooks as lacemakers, while in 1861 William Johnson appears as a silk maker.[5] The workers in these factories were the first occupants of the new housing developed around 1850 in Spital, buyers encouraged by the new savings banks and building societies. The larger houses on Stanley Street and Hartington Road were for the gentlemen owners of the factories. One, in Pigot's *National Commercial Directory* of 1828-29, names its occupant as a Mr Steade of Spital.[6] These houses and the terraced houses around them at the junction of Hartington Road, Valley Road and Stanley Street covered the original area of Spital. On lands once green, streets appeared, and Hady and Spital began to take on a changed aspect (Figures 4-5). The larger houses were big enough to need servants. Hady Farm employed Mary Ann Haines as a house servant, Elizabeth Thornton as dairy maid, and James Norris, a carter. The large house on Hady Hill, owned by the Chesterfield solicitor John Drabble, had its own cook, and several other servants. Catherine Mason and Jemma Andrews, both from Leicester, served in the house of clergyman John Boyer, who lived at Spital House in 1861.

The lace mill at Spital, owned by Messrs Smith & Holmes, was a well run establishment and had an eye to the welfare of the boy and girl workers, who were kept separate. Adults worked in shifts from 4.am onwards. The factory employed four boys as threaders, three ladies over eighteen years old, plus a boy helper and five girls between ten and fourteen as 'winders off'. The work was hard, children were often ill due to the conditions, in spite of improvements brought in under the *Factory Acts*. By 1851 the mill employed 119 people, but trade was declining.

Clayton's Tannery, originally located in Spa Lane, was so successful due to the demand for leather harnesses, shoes, and boots, that new premises were opened on the Horse Croft, which was later to become Clayton Street. Roy Cooper's *Book of Chesterfield* shows several trades in its table of occupations, the highest number being boot and shoe makers, with 40 following the trade in 1833, and 43 in 1846.[7] In modern times, the tannery supplied the leather for the boat used by sailor-author Tim Severin for his 'Brendan Voyage' – later celebrated in his book of the same name - when he tried to prove that Irish monks could have crossed the Atlantic centuries ago in leather boats of this kind.[8] With the introduction of railways in the Victorian era the demand for local leather goods was reduced, but Clayton's Tannery survived and is still a successful company today (Figure 6).

Figure 6. Joseph Clayton's Tannery on Clayton Street, formerly Horse Croft. The tannery is on the right of the picture. *Dennis Middleton*

Mason's tobacco works was another company employing local workers. In the census of 1871, Edwin Mason is shown as providing work for forty-six people, in what must have been a large industrial enterprise. Samuel Shepley also appears as 'clerk in tobacco factory', and Mary Artle as a 'wrapper, layer at the tobacco factory'. William Artle, father of Mary, William Cockshott, Edward Siddall, Samuel Naylor and a young George Mason were also listed as employees at the factory in 1871.[9]

Oliver's Victoria Foundry, the largest iron works in Chesterfield, was bought in 1889 by C P Markham, whose factory produced colliery furnaces, and – much later – tunnelling machinery used in the Channel Tunnel. A great achievement by the Chesterfield firm, which unfortunately is no longer in business. Another iron foundry, that of Joseph Wharton, was situated on Spital Bridge, using the river as a power source. Wharton's name can be seen on iron gates and manhole covers in Spital, and the firm probably made many of the iron railings atop the garden walls, later to be utilised by the army in two world wars for the production of ammunition.

For the lucky children of well to do families, an Academy was established at Spital Lodge by the Atkinson family, which they named the Classical, Mathematical & Commercial Academy. Miss Barbara Russell, listed as schoolmistress in 1871, came from London to teach. Her pupils included Elizabeth Hall and her sister Kate, and Emmeline Wharton was one of the teachers, her own sister Mary Ann Wharton being a pupil, as were the Mason children.[10]

Unfortunately, one result of this influx of new housing, with a close-packed population, was the spread of disease. Sewers, inadequately built for overcrowded houses and yards, could not take the amount of effluent from additional buildings, and there was a serious cholera outbreak. This was probably the worst Spital had suffered since the lethal visit of bubonic plague in 1608, but this time the inhabitants themselves were the cause.

From 1858 onwards, Spital Cemetery was the resting place for those who succumbed. Built on the junction of Hady Hill, Picadilly and Spital Lane, it forms part of a crossroads (Figures 7-8). Within the cemetery are many large family tombs and gravestones. One such tomb is of the Harrison family, which shows that nine children died within days of each other, quite possibly from cholera (Figure 9). Other names are well known, and crop up in census forms and parish registers. One such grave is that of Antonio de Silva, who devoted

Figure 7. Spital Cemetery, Hady Hill. *Dennis Middleton*

Figure 8. Cemetery Chapel, Spital Cemetery. *Dennis Middleton*

Figure 9. Memorial stone at Priest's grave, Spital Cemetery. *Dennis Middleton*

himself to his patients during the influenza epidemic of 1918. Another is that of Sergeant William Coffey, holder of the Victoria Cross, who died a pauper from drink in 1875, unable to forget his dark wartime memories. His headstone was erected in our own day, by members of his regiment.

Other occupants of the cemetery are possibly smallpox victims, who were cared for at the isolation hospital at the far side of Spital on the boundary with Hasland, at Dingle Bank. This hospital, demolished years ago, was visited by relatives who left food at the entrance, washing their hands at the stone trough on Hady Lane, now a part of a wall, to prevent the spread of infection. This piece of oral history, related by local people and the late Farmer Smith, gives a picture of a wooden building, roofed with corrugated iron. The isolation would have been complete, as few buildings stood in the locality in the later nineteenth century. The ambulance driver and cook at the hospital were a husband and wife, Mr and Mrs Hardy. Their descendants now live in Alexandra Road East, in the house previously owned by Mr Mason.

The gatehouse to the cemetery, the lodge, is the second building on the site. The previous old building was used as a threadmill by Page & Co. The three-storeyed building, on the main Chesterfield-Bolsover road, must have been solidly constructed to withstand the heavy iron machinery (Figure 10). Its manager, Mr J Marriott, lived with the caretaker. The old house had an evil reputation, and was said to be haunted:

> *After nightfall children and the timid would not pass it if they could help it. Up to recent times the house was known locally as 'Boggart House' and local stories used to be related of the ghost of a cowled figure with horribly distorted features, which used to be seen in Spital Lane, near the hospital.*[11]

However, all was not suffering and hardship. Spital inhabitants – well, the men anyway – managed to lighten their hardworking days by forming a football team. Founded in 1838, the Spital Football Club held its meetings at the *Eagle Hotel* on Beetwell Street, with dressing rooms at the *Horns Inn* on Lordsmill Street, and played at the Spital ground wearing a strip of blue and white. Many of the committee's names can be found in the census returns as inhabitants of Spital, with Edwin Mason as chairman. For several years the team played successfully against neighbouring sides, having many local

Figure 10. Spital Lodge, Spital Cemetery. *Dennis Middleton*

Figure 11. View from top of Alexandra Road East, location of the Lewis guns in the Second World War. *Dennis Middleton*

business men as members.

Life went on with daily routines, until the day when the dark war clouds appeared. Like any other community in England, Spital had to organise itself against possible enemy bombing. Sheffield, after all, was only a stone's throw away, and its steel works were prime targets for the German bombers. Much closer to home was the engineering works of Bryan Donkin, and not until later was it discovered that the enemy held detailed drawings of the works and its layout. Spital rallied to the cause, the ARP warden's post was set up on Stanley Street, Anderson shelters were allocated, and steel tables provided shelters inside the homes. Fine as protection against bombs, but bad for stubbed toes! Communal shelters on Hollis Lane and Spital were filled with nervous neighbours when the sirens sounded.

On a high point at the top of Alexandra Road East three Lewis guns searched the sky, ready to protect the neighbourhood. Known to the Germans, these guns were manned by soldiers, helped by local boys who carried their ammunition up the steep hill. Probably their reward was the wood from the dismantled gun shelter for the eventual VE Day bonfire (Figure 11). The children of Spital would have had a few new playmates with the evacuees from London, sent to safer areas. Their memories would be worth hearing. One eye-witness recalls:

> *The blackout caused total confusion, especially at the junction of Stanley Road, Alexandra Road East, Valley Road and Hartington Road. One night Father Pickles of St Leonard's Mission Church was heard calling 'Somebody help me, I'm lost!*[12]

The schools in the area also played their part in the war effort. Classes from Hipper and Hady learnt fire practice and gas mask drill, even growing their own vegetables in the grounds of Brambling House, whilst their parents were encouraged to 'dig for victory' in the allotments and back gardens of Spital, growing whatever they could.

On the night of 14 December 1941, a clear moonlit night, patrols spotted parachutes drifting down towards Bolsover, causing fear amongst locals. However, in a lighter vein, the author was told by an elderly lady that: 'A parachute silk made a lovely wedding dress should a girl be lucky enough to get her hands on one.'[13]

The V E Day parties held in 1945 were the reward for a long period of worry, fear and hardship. Many heartwarming memories are recalled of wartime as a time of caring neighbours who were always ready to share what little they had, cups of rationed tea, and telegrams arriving, often with bad news. The cenotaph at Spital Mission Church lists the men of Spital who went to war and never returned. Eighteen in the 1914-18 war, and ten in 1939-45. Spital will always be grateful to them for their ultimate sacrifice.

Since those days, Spital has changed greatly, and continues to do so today. Such is life.

Where once the lace mill stood is the Spital Tile Company's bathroom showroom and sales office (Figure 12). The railway bridge

Figure 12. Spital Tile Company showroom and office, former site of the lace mill. *Dennis Middleton*

Figure 13. New houses on Hady Hill/Picadilly Road, probable site of St Leonard's Leper Hospital. *Dennis Middleton*

has been demolished to widen the road, and Spring Vale houses are long gone. Wharton's ironworks has been replaced by a chapel, once redundant but now reused as a veterinary surgeon's practice. On the formerly thriving factory site of Markham & Co, only the office fronting on to Hollis Lane remains. Behind it the land is occupied by the newly erected Riverside Village housing estate, and once again the road is being changed and widened. The disused football pitch became a cricket pitch for a local team. Now, criss-crossed by children going to school, the haunt of teenagers and dog-walkers, it retains its communal use.

Hady Hill and Spital Lane, once tracks, are both now wide, busy roads. The cemetery sleeps many more than before, and across the road where once the lepers resided, stands a row of new houses (Figure 13). The peace of lepers has been disturbed by progress.

Houses, lorries, cars, televisions, all the bustle of the twenty-first century. A far cry from the quiet fields of long ago.

Notes and References

1. J M Bestall, *History of Chesterfield*, Vol.1 'Early and Medieval Chesterfield', 1974, Chesterfield Borough Council, p 43, pp 105-106.
2. *Derby Mercury*, 3 September 1801.
3. *Ibid*.
4. Roy Cooper, *The Book of Chesterfield*, 1977, Barracuda, p 60.
5. Spital Census 1841 HO 107/194/6 Folios 5-6; Spital Census 1861, RG9/2530 Folios 100-103.
6. Pigot & Co, *National Commercial Directory*, 1828-29 p 121.
7. Roy Cooper, *The Book of Chesterfield*, 1977, Barracuda.
8. Tim Severin, *The Brendan Voyage*, 1978, Hutchinson.
9. Spital Census 1871, Folios 7-9.
10. *Ibid*.
11. T P Wood's *Almanac*, 1935.
12. Fred Harcourt, 'Oral reminiscences of Spital residents' by Spital Local History Group, 2000.
13. Beryl Thompson, *Ibid*.

9. THE RAGGED SCHOOL, CHESTERFIELD

by David Botham

Suffer the little children to come unto me and forbid them not,
for of such is the kingdom of God
Mark Ch. 10 v. 14

'THAT RAGGED SCHOOL down on Markham Road, what is it?'
(Figure 1).

People ask this question so often that I really must start by putting
the answer down in print.

Those who know it best just call it 'chapel'. I tell people that on
Sundays there is a family service at 10.45 am and a traditional gospel
service at 6.30 pm. On Tuesdays and Thursdays there are youth
meetings. Every Thursday there is also Bible study from 7.45 pm and
on Fridays Chesterfield Mission Choir meet from 7.30 pm. In the
Upper Room, Acorn Christian Ministries run a variety of youth
orientated activities.

By now, the enquirer has had time to frame the question that lay
behind the first and they usually interject

'Yes, but how did it get that name?'

Figure 1. The Ragged School, 2002, photographed from Park Road.
Dennis Middleton

Figure 2. Dog Kennels alleyway viewed from Castle Yard *c.*1911 (the chapel east side can be glimpsed behind the sewer vent. *Author's collection*

Once there were many Ragged Schools. They were essentially free Sunday schools run by volunteers. They were set up in the poorer parts of Victorian industrial towns and cities for children who might otherwise never darken the doors of a church or school. Characters from Dickens or Kingsley, slaving in mills or maybe sweeping chimneys the hard way. Ragged Schools were for ragged children (Figure 2).

'So why build it where there are no houses?'

When Chesterfield's Ragged School opened there was no traffic thundering by. There was no Markham Road, New Beetwell Street, bus stand or car park. The townscape consisted of a rabbit warren of

Map Extracts, 1827 & 1837

(a) 1827
George Glossop jnr
scale 1"= 214'

Figure 3. Map Extract, 1827 (George Glossop) and 1837 (Jonas Chapman).

Chesterfield Borough Council

narrow alleyways running south from the Market Place right down to the banks of the River Hipper (Figure 3). This pattern had its origins in the burgage plots of the medieval market. Originally there would have been just the house, shop or inn fronting the market with outbuildings and a smallholding to the rear. For six hundred years the layout hardly changed.[1] Then the industrial revolution reached Chesterfield.

Alongside the meandering river a variety of industrial concerns were already established by the time of Potter's survey in 1803. On the Ragged School site a carpet factory is marked. By 1837, this had been replaced with a square block corresponding to the size and shape of the present main building (Figure 4). There is evidence that this may have been a purpose built mill to house John Waterhouse's great lace making machine. The chapel deeds do not mention names, but the date and style of construction are a good match. Records of the inventor's move to Wheeldon Lane are confirmed in trade directories.[2] In 1849 a John Thackery was running the mill. By 1851 it was up for sale. George Mason appears to have bought the building for his tobacco and pipe manufacturing until he moved to his larger, purpose built factory near the railway.

Throughout the nineteenth century, maps of the town show gardens and orchards disappearing under tightly packed rows of cheap terraced housing and small factories. The area began to acquire a doubtful reputation. Policemen were instructed not to venture down the 'long yards' alone.

Four young men from the nearby Congregational Church resolved that something should be done for the families that had to live in such a place. Seeking premises, they found the former factory on Wheeldon Lane vacant. The previous tenants had run a beer and lodging house of such ill-repute that the authorities had closed it down. The mission team duly rented the upper room and opened for the first time on Sunday, 28 July 1878.[3] One hundred and nine children came that morning. The four teachers enlisted more help. After two weeks, an afternoon meeting was added. After three weeks, an evening gospel service was held, attended by fifty adults.

The mission continued to grow. A teachers' meeting was inaugurated to govern the school. Minutes of the first meeting are dated 30 October 1878. On May 5 1879, the Ragged School became a member of the Chesterfield Sunday School Union.

Public support for the work, especially from other churches, was generous. Denominational differences were put aside as donations of books, food and other gifts were sent. The founders seem to have

Map Extract, 1878 1:500

Figure 4. Map Extract, 1878. Reproduced from Ordnance Survey Sheet XXV.6.14. Scale 1:500. *Ordnance Survey; Chesterfield Borough Council*

⌐ RULES. ⌐

1.—That during prayers all talking shall cease throughout the School, and reverence shown by the closing of eyes and bowed heads (except teachers). The old scholars showing a good example to the others in this respect, both male and female.

2.—That all boys remember that the School is a Place of Worship, and therefore no hat or cap is to be worn after entering the lobby.

3.—That no girl or boy shall move from one class to another without permission of the Superintendent.

4.—That everyone shall remain seated until their star card be given them, and not stand upon the seats, or struggle in any way to obtain it.

5.—That all the classes shall wait in the lower hall until their teacher goes upstairs, and not make a disturbance by going before him or her to their respective rooms.

6.—That all teachers shall be in their places at 10.25 a m. and 2.25 p.m., so that they may be with their scholars at the opening of school.

7.—That every assistance be given to the Superintendent in obtaining and maintaining silence and good order during the opening and closing of school. Teachers shall not hesitate to move from their accustomed places to quell a disturbance in any part of the school.

8.—That all teachers get possession of names and addresses of their scholars so that visits may be made in sickness or absence for any other cause.

9.—That if any teacher be away for one Sunday, they are expected to notify the Superintendent and if at all possible provide a substitute.

10.—That if any teacher be away from his or her class for four consecutive Sundays without a reasonable cause, that person must not expect to resume the teachings of his or her original class.

11.—That scholars remember that the persistent breaking of their rules will make a material difference in their prize.

12.—That the Superintendent read over the rules to the school, the first Sunday of each month.

Figure 5. School Rules, 1885. *Chesterfield Ragged School Archive*

resolved from the very first that they would devote all available resources to the local work and waste nothing on formal ties with Methodist, Baptist, Congregational or other organisations but rather welcome them all as friends and fellow workers. This remains true today.

The effectiveness of such wholehearted concentration on the job in hand is reflected in the attendance records. By 1885 there were 340 scholars and 27 teachers on the books. More impressive still was the proportion of these who were coming regularly. Average weekly attendances were 319 and 24 respectively.

Discipline must have been very difficult to maintain. The school rules are most illuminating. The requirement that 'Teachers shall not hesitate to move from their accustomed places to quell a disturbance.' (Rule 7) rather suggests that quelling was frequently needed![4] (Figure 5).

Mid-week meetings and social events were soon added to the school's calendar. Band of Hope, Sisterhood, Christian Endeavour, classes of various kinds, Christmas treats, summer trips and games, special mission weeks all gave interest, direction and purpose to the lives of those involved. When it became evident that many of the children were poorly fed and rarely had anything for breakfast, the teachers organised a basic meal before Sunday school. It is not known how many years they were able to continue this kind of help, but it certainly made the place even more popular!

...and from your bounty, O God, you provided for the poor.
Psalm 68 v. 10

Finance was a significant item on the agenda with so many mouths and minds to feed. In such an area, the usual freewill offerings were never going to balance the books, so bazaars and services of song were arranged to which the aldermen and local politicians were invited along with a large proportion of the town's clergy.

Sunday School anniversaries were held. Civic dignitaries and captains of industry were invited to share the platform with the preachers and join the board of trustees or serve a term as president or vice president. Naturally, they were also expected to dig deep when the collecting box came around or letters went out to solicit annual subscriptions or donations to the Christmas Tree Fund. A typical anniversary collection is recorded in the minute book (Figure 6). The

Figure 6. Minutes Book extract (collection).
Chesterfield Ragged School Archive

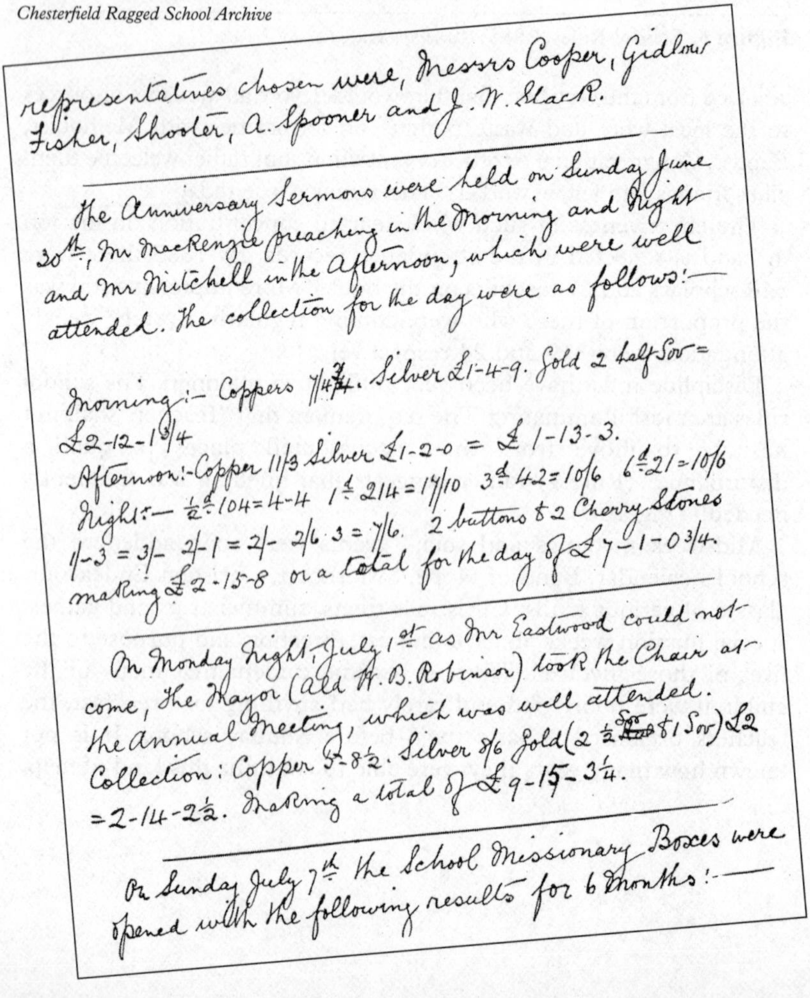

representatives chosen were, Messrs Cooper, Gidlow, Fisher, Shooter, A. Spooner and J. W. Slack.

The Anniversary Sermons were held on Sunday June 30th, Mr MacKenzie preaching in the Morning and Night and Mr Mitchell in the Afternoon, which were well attended. The collection for the day were as follows:—

Morning:— Coppers 7/4¾. Silver £1-4-9. Gold 2 half Sov = £2-12-1¾
Afternoon:- Copper 11/3 Silver £1-2-0 = £1-13-3.
Night:— ½d 104 = 4-4 1d 214 = 17/10 3d 42 = 10/6 6d 21 = 10/6 1/-3 = 3/- 2/-1 = 2/- 2/6 3 = 7/6. 2 buttons & 2 Cherry Stones making £2-15-8 or a total for the day of £7-1-0¾.

On Monday Night, July 1st as Mr Eastwood could not come, The Mayor (Ald W. B. Robinson) took the Chair at the Annual Meeting, which was well attended. Collection: Copper 5-8½. Silver 8/6 Gold (2 ½ Sov & 1 Sov) £2 = 2-14-2½. Making a total of £9-15-3¼.

On Sunday July 7th the School Missionary Boxes were opened with the following results for 6 months:—

boxes used were wooden, which explains the last few items. A button or a cherry stone might be dropped in to pass for the sound of a farthing as long as your neighbours all respected the polite convention of not looking!

After nine years, the work was still growing and the teachers resolved to purchase the whole building. After long negotiations, it was secured for £480. The school did not have any capital and could not borrow but the teachers were confident that the Lord would provide. They launched a public appeal, ran a huge bazaar and by the end of 1891 had raised £280. At the annual general meeting in January 1892, it was announced that an anonymous benefactor had cleared the whole of the remaining debt.

Two hundred pounds was a magnificent sum in such times and in such a community. The question in everyone's mind was 'Who was it?' One suspects that despite the anonymity, he was well known to the teachers and may even have been present at the meeting but although the minutes secretary expressed appropriate gratitude, the secret was never revealed.

Readers today will know little about the pioneers who set up the mission. This may be an appropriate moment to get to know a few of those hardworking and devoted folk who did what they could to bring light where there was darkness and hope where there was despair.

The Spirit of the Lord is upon me, because the Lord has anointed
me to preach good news to the poor
Isaiah 61 v. 1

According to contemporary records, the four men who started the mission were Arthur and Henry Slack, Henry Shaw and Frederick Conroy from Soresby Street Congregational Church. They were joined as soon as the regular meetings began in 1878 by many others, notably Messrs Saunders, Gidlow, Walton, Hadfield and Legge. A stone memorial tablet in the school confusingly records two of the first group and two of the second together.

The Slack brothers contributed much to the Sunday Schools in the town, besides pursuing independent careers in local commerce. Henry, the eldest, also helped found the Salvation Army movement in the town and later became superintendent of Marsden Street Methodist Church. Arthur seems to have taken a more prominent role at the Ragged School, being elected as superintendent in 1879 and continuing in office until 1901. Mr Conroy and Mr Shaw lived to see only the early years, Mr Shaw serving as treasurer from 1880 to 1886.

Frank Saunders was a colporteur. He sold bibles, tracts and Christian literature in the Chesterfield area. He seems to have been a very effective door to door salesman for God and for the Ragged School. It is recorded that in one year alone he sold 1,901 copies of the scriptures, and 5,810 other books besides supplying 1616 magazines and Sunday School cards.

Mr Gidlow was described to me from memory by the chapel's oldest surviving member as a tall, grey-haired figure who was never elected to a principal office but worked as hard as anyone for the school.

One of the best known characters amongst the founders was Thomas Hadfield, the butcher, whose Market Place premises extended right down Castle Yard. His empire included a sausage factory and a tiny square of terraced houses just above the chapel, which was commonly known as 'Hadfield Town'. One might say that Mr Hadfield had a vested interest in establishing a Ragged School literally in his own backyard, but he was a longserving and generous neighbour. When he died in 1903, the school held a memorial service and raised a commemorative plaque. There must have been some benefit to his firm as the business lasted another three generations. I can remember the chapel drains getting blocked by sausages from further up the yard as late as 1960!

> *Continue to live in Him, rooted and built up in Him,*
> *strengthened in the faith as you were taught.*
> Col. 2 vs. 6-7.

The turn of the century heralded great changes in the long yards. Municipal concern was being expressed about the state of the area. The obvious deprivation resulting from over development may have been a significant factor in the renewed determination that the Borough boundaries must be increased and land released for housing and industry.

The first new development in the immediate vicinity of the school was the Queen's Park, officially dedicated on 21 September 1887 in celebration of Victoria's golden jubilee; it was not to be opened to the public until six years later, in 1893.[5] This had been unofficially used by the children for years while it was still Maynard's meadows but now the school had unrestricted access to better facilities. A cricket pitch was added, the first county match being played in June 1898. The River Hipper had already been straightened by the building of the Midland Railway's branch line to Brampton. Now new roads were planned from the town centre. A huge embankment was raised to the west of the chapel with a bridge over Park Road to bring the Lancashire, Derbyshire and East Coast Railway to its terminus in the corner of New Square, opened in 1897 (Figure 7). Finally, in

Figure 7. Map Extract, 1898. Reproduced from Ordnance Survey Sheet XXV.6, 2nd edition. Scale 1:2500. *Ordnance Survey; Chesterfield Borough Council*

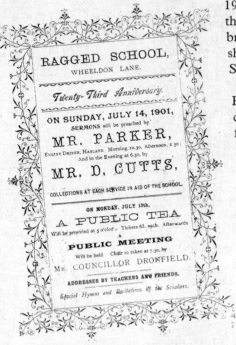

Figure 8. Handbill advertising 'Twenty-Third Anniversary' on 14 July 1901.
Chesterfield Ragged School Archive

1911, Markham Road was built, cutting through the slums from east to west and bringing new houses and rivalry in the shape of the *Queen's Park Hotel* and the Salvation Army Citadel.[6]

Through all the external upheavals the Ragged School prospered. By 1901 the children's mission had grown into a fully-fledged independent church (Figure 8).

Arthur Slack, still a senior deacon at Soresby Street Congregational Church, felt unable to accept this expanding role and resigned from his demanding double office of superintendent and treasurer. Frank Saunders was elected as the new superintendent with the support of James Davenport as secretary, Robert Fisher as treasurer, and the distinguished figure of Mr W Marples.

When Mr Saunders left the district in 1908, Mr Davenport took his place while Mr Marples took over as secretary. This dedicated pair held the chapel fellowship on course through the storms of two world wars and more changes than they could possibly have imagined.

May the God of Peace......equip you with everything
good for doing His will.
Heb. ch.13 v. 20

By this time, the old converted factory was full to overflowing. Between the turn of the century and the Second World War there were over 400 scholars on the books. Anniversary services had to be organised on a rota basis over two Sundays to allow every child a turn in the singing. With no grant aid or national church to support them, the teachers kept the work going through world war and economic depression, not by believing in miracles, but by relying on them.

When Markham Road was opened, a new frontage to the chapel site was created. Alderman E Eastwood, founder of the town's railway wagon works and president of the chapel, pledged £100 to start a fund to build a new schoolroom for the younger children

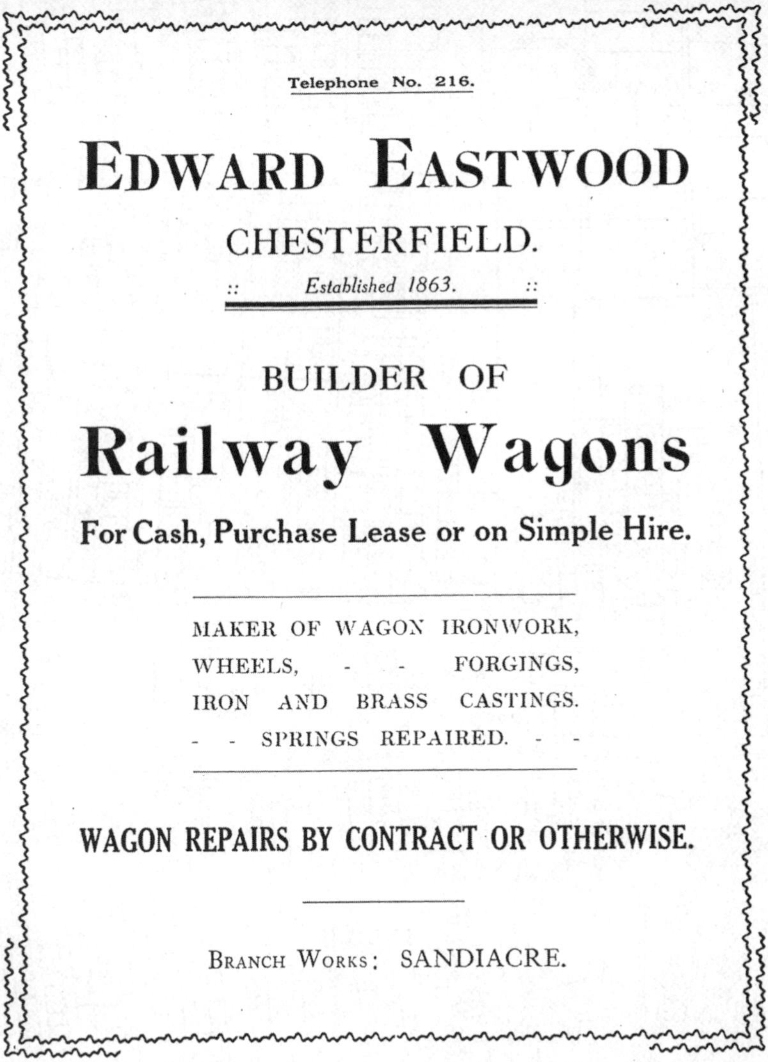

Figure 9. Advertisement for Eastwood's Company (wagon builders). *Author's collection*

(Figure 9). When he died in 1910, his son, Alderman G A Eastwood, took his place and championed the scheme as a memorial to his father. At the stonelaying ceremony reported in the *Derbyshire Courier,* July 1914, he observes that the Borough Council were obliged to charge for the extra land needed. However, he then invited all the councillors and officials to the ceremony, seeking subscriptions to the cause to such good effect that their collective generosity paid back the whole of the land costs![7]

The builder, David Brown of Hasland, completed the job in four months, with extras totalling just nine shillings and fourpence.

Sadly, events of worldwide significance overshadowed what should

Figure 10. Map Extract, 1914. Reproduced from Ordnance Survey Sheet XXV.6, 3rd edition. Scale 1:2500. *Ordnance Survey; Chesterfield Borough Council*

Figure 11. Whit Walk *c.*1910, showing Ragged School marching up St Mary's Gate. *Author's collection*

have been the chapel's finest hour. Within weeks, the government requisitioned the whole premises to provide barracks for the Lancashire Fusiliers while they were billeted in the town (Figure 10).

Undaunted, the teachers temporarily transferred their classes to Hipper Street Junior school. Eight months later, they were able to return to the Ragged School and complete their infants' accommodation by adding a platform.

Special efforts seem to have been made to maintain all services and children's treats throughout the war. Alderman Shentall (later to be knighted) maintained his annual gifts of fir trees at Christmas and oranges at Whitsuntide (Figures 11 & 12). This was more than

Figure 12. Whit Walk *c.*1910, marching down Park Road from New Square (led by Mr Marples). *Author's collection*

generous under the circumstances for there were close on 500 children and teachers and Sir Ernest always sent enough for everyone.

As the war dragged on, the young men of the chapel were called one by one to serve in the forces. Teachers arranged to send them parcels and gifts. A roll of honour was drawn up recording all who went out.

Alderman Eastwood continued his active support as president, promising a treat for the whole school whenever peace should be declared. Peace was a long time coming but the president kept his promise and threw a memorable party for the entire school at Brambling House.

The end of the war was also however a time for counting the cost. Two families who had worked hard for the children lost sons on the battlefields of France. George Shooter and Sam May did not return and the third minute book concludes with the poignant arrangements for Sam's memorial service.

When I needed a neighbour, were you there?

Ever practical, when the question of a permanent memorial was raised, the members resolved to collect a hundred pounds and invest it in corporation housing bonds. The interest was to be distributed annually to deserving cases.

Hard times in war were followed by hard times in peace. The memorial fund target was not reached until 1921 and for many years the chapel distributed much more to deserving cases than the interest from the bonds. The town's Education Committee set up a scheme to feed needy children. They asked if the Ragged School could be used as a distribution centre and the members willingly agreed.

Small wonder that with so much to do, the remainder owed to the bank for the new schoolroom didn't get back on the agenda until 1923, when a concerted effort was made to clear the debt and also install electricity. The teachers raised £50 in time for the annual general meeting of 1924 at which it was announced that a £100 bequest had reduced the amount owing to just £4. Typically, Alderman Eastwood promptly paid this out of his own pocket, bringing his task as building fund treasurer to a fitting end.

A year earlier, in 1923, the school enjoyed an unexpected bit of public recognition for its work when the Duke of Devonshire's eldest daughter, Lady Maud Mackintosh, visited the chapel with her fiancé. Her recorded reaction to the scale and success of the school was that it was an 'absolute revelation' and her congratulations to the officers and volunteers was well reported in the local press.[8]

The 50th Jubilee celebrations in 1928 brought further publicity and encouragement. With such support, the teachers took stock of the old building and embarked on major improvements including replacement windows and the installation of a two manual pipe organ from Brampton Congregational Church. At the re-opening services in October 1930, the secretary happily records that every available seat was filled.

There were calls in the following year for a fund to be started to install central heating in the main building, but there seems to have been little enthusiasm for taking on another challenge so soon. The regular work was demanding enough with 460 children on the books at the end of 1933. Four cast iron radiators were eventually added to the existing system to serve the back room, but the main room continued to rely on an open fire and a 'turtle' stove for heating for another fifty years. The clank of galvanised buckets of coke and the acrid whiff of burning were a regular feature of winter services until 1988.

The first annual general meeting recorded in the fifth volume of the minutes books was overshadowed by the passing of the school's president.

Alderman G Eastwood had been a tower of strength to the chapel through difficult times. The whole assembly stood in silent tribute. The sympathy and appreciation expressed were duly followed by calls for Miss Blanche Eastwood to be invited to take her father's place. Her acceptance carried her family's presidency into a third generation and gave a measure of stability through the uncertain years that were to follow.

At the 1936 meeting, appreciation was again expressed when it was announced that the long serving assistant superintendent, Walter Wicks, had been made both an alderman and a justice of the peace. There was unusual warmth in the congratulations for Mr Wicks was a popular teacher and musician, training and conducting the children for anniversaries since before the First World War. He had a special rapport with the scholars who would follow him out into the park after the services in scenes reminiscent of the Pied Piper of Hamelin. His leadership in Sunday school and music helped the chapel through the dark years of another world war

In 1942, following the evacuation from Dunkirk, the government again requested help in finding accommodation for troops. This time, the matter was approached on a more reasonable footing, the authorities asking for the Eastwood Room only and offering a rent of £40 p.a. for the duration. The contingent settled in for a couple of years, building themselves a rough kitchen and wash-house in the rear yard which was eventually sold to the school for £30 and served as a store for another fifty years.

The Sunday School infants department had to be crammed into the Endeavour Room. Small children were sat in every windowsill and squashed into every corner. Nevertheless, the few remaining teachers managed to keep classes going and even found time to organise occasional entertainment for the troops.

On the conclusion of hostilities, there were thanksgivings, reunions, joys and sadness, but in the autumn of 1945, the deepest sense of loss did not arise from a casualty of war. Walter Wicks, having led the Borough Council's 'Dig for Victory' campaign on the allotments and proudly seen so many of his former pupils acquit themselves well in adversity, did not live to see all of them return to his beloved Ragged School. There were tributes recorded for his contribution to all kinds of good work in the town.

In retrospect, it seems that his passing signified the end of an era in the chapel's history.

> *We will tell the next generation the praiseworthy deeds of the Lord,*
> *His power and the wonders He has done.*
> Psalm 78 v. 4

When the Second World War came to an end, a new age dawned for many peoples and nations. How did a Victorian mission to the poor come to terms with the atomic bomb, the welfare state and social housing which spread even the poorest families out across large estates of three bedroom, semi-detached houses?

The rest of the country's Ragged Schools have vanished almost without trace, made redundant by state education and higher standards of living.

One must also admit that the name has associations with the poverty of a bygone age. In the 1950s it lacked a modern image. In ensuing decades it wasn't 'trendy', 'groovy', or 'cool'. People didn't choose to attend the Ragged School if they were social climbers or status seekers. Perhaps this was a hidden blessing, testing the humility of those who continued to cross the threshold, but all things considered, Chesterfield's school is an amazing survival. Why is it still there?

One essential factor to date has been the ongoing process of change and renewal, both in the building and the people. The Spirit that moved the founders is still at work.

In the 1950s, the new superintendent, Cliff Tingay, and secretary, Geoff Collins, worked hard to meet changing needs and tackle major building repairs including roof, gable wall and organ re-building.

Figure 13a & b. Choir Christmas card cover illustrations. *Author's collection*

Omega & Alpha He
Let the organ thunder!

Officers of the Ragged School, Chesterfield, 1878-1998

(date first elected shown in brackets)

Superintendent	Secretary	Treasurer	President	Notes
Mr. J. Walton 30/10/1878 Mr. A. Slack 8/1/79	Mr. J. Butcher 30/10/1878	Mr. T. Hadfield 30/10/1878 Mr. H. Shaw 13/1/80	Mr. J. Walton 8/1/79	Librarian was a key support worker for first 30 years. The following served. Mr. Legge '79 onwards
	Mr. Buxton 12/1/82			
Assistant Supt. also appointed in these years. Mr. Legge 85/86 Mr. Dronfield '89 Mr. F. Saunders '90	Mr. H. Wilde 23/7/85	Mr. A. Slack 13/10/86	Ald. E. Eastwood 14/1/89	Mr Wilcockson '92 Mr W Slack '93 Mr. J. Shooter '95 onwards
	Mr. J. Wilcockson 28/1/90 Mr. T. Hadfield 19/1/92 Mr. J.W. Slack 14/2/95			
Mr. F. Saunders 15/4/1901 Mr. J. Davenport 26/11/08	Mr. J. Davenport 15/4/1901 Mr. W. Marples 26/11/08	Mr. R. Fisher 15/4/1901 Mr. W. Marples 12/2/1902 Mr. Turner 26/11/08 Mr. W. Milner 10/2/09	(d. June 1910) Mr. G. Eastwood 14/11/10	Mr. W. Holland 1914 [1st World War]
Mr. H. Gidlow 1914 Mr. R. Fisher 2/12/15 Mr. W. Wicks 1919 Mr. J. Davenport 4/2/19		Mr. T. Wicks 15/2/37 Mr. P. Wicks 13/3/40 Mr. W. Marples 19/3/41 Mr. S. Hooper 10/3/48	Miss B. Eastwood 18/2/35	[2nd World War]
Mr. C. Tingay 1945 Mr. G. Collins 1949 Mr. C. Tingay 14/2/49	Mr G. Collins 22/3/54			
Mr. F. Montgomery 1959	Mr J.W. Short 13/3/61 Miss L. Maycock 2/5/66		Cllr. E.C. Hancock 16/3/64	
(Post re-defined & designated "Pastor") Mr. N. Siddon 7/3/88	Mr D.F. Botham 2/4/76	Mr. J. Baxter 28/11/77		
(2002 update) Development Leader appointed 2/02 Mr. D. Bayden	continuing	continuing	vacant	

Figure 14. Principal Officers of the Ragged School, 1878-1998. *Chesterfield Ragged School Archive*

In the 1970s and 80s, the threat of compulsory purchase, followed by another cycle of repairs and improvements encouraged teamwork in practical as well as spiritual matters for the next generation. The last of the town centre family housing has disappeared but the car parks and buses are still there for those willing to switch off their televisions and get back in touch with their Maker. Even as I write, the present fellowship is experiencing a further time of renewal, seeking to meet the spiritual needs of a new millennium (Figure 13a & b).

As long as this pattern continues there will always be another chapter of history to write (Figure 14).

Acknowledgements

I would like to thank everyone who shared a memory, passed on a photograph, or imparted a vital bit of information. It would be impossible to list every name but the following deserve a special mention. Past and present members of the Ragged School, including the secretaries who carefully minuted each meeting and kept the records intact. Chesterfield Library and Chesterfield Borough Council whose staff have kindly permitted me to copy illustrations from their archives.

Notes and References

1. J M Bestall, *History of Chesterfield,* Vol. I 'Early and Medieval Chesterfield', 1974 pp 132-134.
2. Bagshaw's *Directory of Derbyshire,* 1846 p.623.
3. *Derbyshire Courier,* 3 August 1878.
4. Ragged School Rules, 1885.
5. T F Wright, *History of Chesterfield* Vol IV The Growth of the Modern Town, 1851-1939 p.54; Sadler, Geoff, *Queen's Park: the First Sixty Years, 1887-1947,* pp 1-2.
6. T F Wright, *ibid,* pp 147-148.
7. *Derbyshire Times,* 18 July 1914.
8. *Derbyshire Times,* 3 November 1923.

10. CHESTERFIELD: AN UNEXPECTED THEATRE TOWN

by Lynne Patrick

CHESTERFIELD IS NOT EXACTLY THE FIRST TOWN that comes to mind in any list of theatrical hotbeds – yet live theatre has flourished here for centuries, and shows every sign of continued wellbeing. There is clear evidence of the existence of a theatre in the early 1600s, when the first Theatre Royal was built on what is now Theatre Yard. The site was provided by the Foljambes, an influential family in the town still commemorated in several street names; Theatre Yard is now a shopping area but at one time was also the location of a fire station and a police institute[1] (Figure 1). As recently as the mid-nineteenth century the theatre occasionally hosted leading professional companies, but fell victim to poor management and failing audiences (Figure 2).

Figure 1. Map showing the Theatre Royal in Theatre Yard. Reproduced from Ordnance Survey Sheet XXV.6.9 (1:500 scale), 1878. *Chesterfield Local Studies Library*

CHESTERFIELD, October 16th, 1786.

Mr. DREWRY,

Please to insert the following Epilogue, entitled, " The Progress of the Drama," written by Mr. D. Deacon, jun. and spoken by Mr. Venables, at the New Theatre in Chesterfield, on Saturday the 14th Inst. which gave universal Satisfaction ; and no doubt, if it appears in your Mercury, will prove acceptable to many of your Readers. I am yours, &c.

THE STAGE has been, from earliest Times, design'd
  A School to soften and sublime the Mind.
Where the sweet Muse displays her mimic Art,
To fire with Virtue, and expand the Heart,
To melt with Pity, bid the Tear to flow,
And rend the Bosom for another's Woe.
Where, led by Wisdom's all-directive Power,
She traces Nature thro' her secret Bower,
To Folly's Eye th' awak'ning Scene unfolds,
And up to Vice, the faithful Mirror holds.
  Such is the Drama's Theme, that draws her Rise
From Grecia's hallow'd Soil ; and still supplies
The World with Pleasure—still its Praises meets,
Perpetual Fountains of exhaustless Sweets !
  At first, with feeble Lustre, she appear'd,
And by Degrees her mighty Fabric rear'd.
Now mark her Progress ! See, her mimic Strain,
At Athen's fam'd, redoubled Strength attain,
And blaze with bright Effulgence—now inspire
With Comic Vein, and now, with Tragic Fire.
But ah ! the Instability of Things,
That alters Empires, and the Lines of Kings !
  Not there content to fix eternal Seat,
(Tho' lov'd by all) she took a sad Retreat,
Forsook th' Athenian all-enlighten'd Dome,
And plac'd her Dwelling at imperial Rome.
There long she dwelt ; till Luxury and War,
Impell'd her thence deplum'd, to wander far !
And long she travers'd many a dreary Coast,
Sometimes in Monkish Cells and Cloisters lost.
At length she rous'd, beheld her Shakespeare smile,
And fell well-pleas'd on England's happy Isle.
Joy'd with the beauteous Land, devoid of Fear,
She cried,—" Fair Place ! my Residence is here !"
  Nor are confin'd to London's lofty Towers
Her dulcet Favors and delightful Powers ;
At CHESTERFIELD, behold the Muse embrac'd,
The Place of Science and superior Taste,
Where Wit and Beauty, Sense and Candor shine,
And noble Actions speak their Breasts benign.
No wonder, that the Goddess deigns to come,
Where all these Virtues so conspicuous bloom.
Nor will she quit, in Haste, this happy Vale,
(If Truth inspires the sacred Muse's Tale)
While HUNLOKE smiles, while Taste and Genius grace
The gen'rous Patrons of this lovely Place,
While pleas'd, around, with voluntary Choice,
Enchanting Beauties give th' applausive Voice.

Figure 2. Poem *The Progress of the Drama* by Mr D Deacon, Jr, read by Mr Venables on 14 October 1786 at the New Theatre, Chesterfield (Theatre Royal). *Derby Mercury, 16 October 1786*

By the start of the 1900s, Corporation Street at the other side of town was already gaining a reputation as the town's entertainment centre. A hundred years later the area reverberates with the sound of music from the succession of night clubs which has sprung up, and entertainment has come to mean something different. But in the first decade of the twentieth century, when flashing lights and electronic amplification had not even entered the imagination of science fiction writers, a night out often meant the theatre or music hall.

When the century turned the Hippodrome occupied the corner opposite what is now the Pomegranate. Music hall was at the height of its popularity, and for the first three decades of the twentieth century large crowds enjoyed the rumbustious variety evenings.

The Corporation Theatre opened in 1904 to provide a venue for the higher forms of cultural entertainment. Mr F R Benson's Shakespearean Company became periodic visitors, as did various local amateur companies.[2] Subscription concerts also formed a regular part of the programme (Figures 3-4).

On Burlington Street, just a

CORPORATION THEATRE, CHESTERFIELD.

The North of England Theatre Corporation, Limited.
Lessees
Managing Director   Mr. FRANK MACNAGHTEN.
Resident Manager   Mr. G. M. DICKINSON.

MR. F. R. BENSON'S SHAKESPEAREAN COMPANY.

Programme.

Merry Wives of Windsor.

Sir John Falstaff	Mr. HENRY HERBERT
Fenton	Mr. GERALD AMES
Shallow, a Country Justice	Mr. LIONEL BEVANS
Slender, his Cousin	Mr. A. FAYNE
Ford — Two Gentlemen	Mr. BERNARD LIMPUS
Page — living in Windsor	Mr. CHARLES FRANCIS
Sir Hugh Evans, a Welsh Priest	Mr. MONTAGUE WIGAN
Dr. Caius, a French Physician	Mr. ALFRED HARRIS
Host of the " Garter " Inn	Mr. JAMES ANNAND
Robin, a Page of Falstaff	Miss LOUISE GRAEME
Bardolph — Followers	Mr. HODGKINS
Pistol — of	Mr. GERALD
Nym — Falstaff	Mr. BARBER
	Mr. ROSS SHORE
Simple, Servant to Slender	Mr. WILSON
Rugby, Servant to Dr. Caius	Miss DOROTHY GREEN
Mrs. Ford	Miss KATE TURNER
Mrs. Page	Miss DULCIE GREATWICH
Anne Page	Miss MAY DE LAUNEY
Mistress Quickley	

Tuesday, DEC. 12th, at 7.45

Figure 3. Poster advertising a performance by Mr Benson and Company at the Corporation Theatre. *Chesterfield Local Studies Library*

Figure 4. Concert performance by local pianist Katie Bacon at the Corporation Theatre. She also played the Whigmore and New York Philharmonic Hall. *Chesterfield Local Studies Library*

In Aid of the Prince of Wales' National Relief Fund.

CORPORATION THEATRE, CHESTERFIELD,
(Kindly lent by the Directors).

WEDNESDAY, SEPTEMBER 16th, at 3-15 p.m.

Grand Pianoforte and Vocal Recital

Miss Katie Bacon.   Mr. Roland Jackson (Tenor).

Accompanist   -   Mr. J. FREDERIC STATON, Mus. Bac.

minute's walk from the theatres, was the town's own Picture Palace.[3] Film was still in its infancy, but silent movies were a popular outing; and at Christmas the screen was packed away and lively, colourful pantomimes attracted large audiences.

At the other end of town, the West Bars skating rink provided a large-capacity venue for boxing matches, concerts and festivals in addition to its prime function.

So theatre in one form or another was part of Chesterfield's everyday life in the first half of the twentieth century – but history records only the highlights and low spots. Against a constantly changing background of visiting plays, music hall evenings and silent movies, a handful of moments stand out:

• 1906 was a General Election year, and the Labour Party was beginning to make a mark in Parliament; the Theatre Royal was an ideal choice of venue for campaign meetings. Coincidentally, this was the year of the birth of Hugh Gaitskell, who would become one of the party's greatest leaders.

• Christmas 1911 should have been a happy time at the Picture Palace; the customary seasonal entertainment was taking place, with the usual chorus of girl dancers. But the year ended in tragedy. Open fires were the only source of warmth in the dressing room, and five girls aged between eleven and fourteen died when a costume caught alight; the blaze spread rapidly, causing panic among the cast members. The only escape route was up a narrow staircase: a far cry from the elaborate and well policed safety regulations which protect both cast and audience nowadays. Thirteen-year-old Ada Tidhall heroically turned back to save a trapped friend; her attempt at rescue cost her her own life.[4]

• Twelve years later the young Russian ballerina Anna Pavlova visited Chesterfield as part of a long summer tour. On the afternoon of 18 July 1923 she danced the Dying Swan in a packed Corporation Theatre; one newspaper critic waxed effusively lyrical over her 'unlimited genius and artistic temperament.'[5] Her full schedule took her to Mansfield the same evening.

• Nine years on, the need for proper safety procedures was highlighted once again when the skating rink was destroyed by fire. The building was completely gutted by an inferno which raged throughout the night of 16 February 1932: a date many senior citizens will recall. This time there were no casualties, but houses were endangered on nearby Clarence Road, and as woodwork scorched and windows began to crack a number of families moved to a safe distance. The rink, which had been the town's largest public building since its opening in 1909, was never rebuilt.[6]

World War Two was to prove a major watershed; in cultural and social terms, change was inevitable, and post-war Britain rapidly became a very different place.

Entertainment had moved on; cinema was in the ascendant and the music hall was moribund. In the late 1940s and early 1950s, even visits from big names such as Gracie Fields and Max Bygraves did little to revive the failing fortunes of the Hippodrome, and a venture into the dubious realm of striptease proved no more successful. The theatre finally closed its doors in July 1955.[7] Over the next quarter century there were several attempts to resurrect the building as a sports hall and public meeting place, but the entire site was eventually razed, and became part of the foundations of the new Chesterfield by-pass which opened in 1986.[8]

As the twentieth century moved into its second half, the popularity of stage drama had also seen a decline, and the Stephenson Memorial Hall on Corporation Street had been pressed into service as a cinema. But a pressure group called the Chesterfield Three Arts Society persuaded the Borough Council that there was still a place for live theatrical performance in the town; plans to convert the building into a modern theatre had been proposed as early as 1946. Early in 1949 the work was completed, and the final bill totalled more than £23,000. Running costs had still to be met; even then, live theatre rarely paid for itself. The Arts Council contributed a grant of £3,000, but with conditions: a reserve fund had to be created, sufficient to pay the bills until the new theatre was on its feet. The people of Chesterfield, ever generous, proved enthusiastic, and added nearly £5,400 to the coffers (Figure 5).

Figure 5. Civic Theatre Programme, 1949. *Pomegranate Theatre Archive, on permanent loan to Chesterfield Local Studies Library*

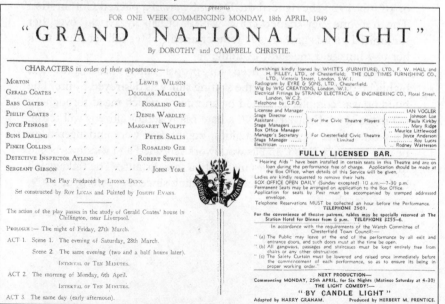

Chesterfield's Civic Theatre, the first council-funded repertory theatre in the country, was formally opened on 19 February 1949 by Kathleen Harrison, a top stage and screen actress of the day, at a ceremony attended by such notable figures as the secretary-general of the Arts Council and playwright Philip King.[9]

King's farce *See How They Run* was the first production by the 23-strong repertory company. Margaret Wolfit, daughter of leading actor-manager Sir Donald was in the cast. Reviews of that first show were lukewarm, and the second production, J B Priestley's *An Inspector Calls,* fared little better. But for the time being audiences were large and enthusiastic, and a month later *The First Mrs Fraser* drew much warmer praise from the critics. In the spring of that year the company took part in a BBC radio series, giving an account of the theatre's origins and presenting some excerpts from *See How They Run* (Figure 6).

Manager Ian Vogler ensured that there was provision for amateur companies as well the resident players. Chesterfield Playgoers, formed in 1933, had been among the prime movers in the bid to

Figure 6. Peter Sallis, a regular cast member, enjoying some female attention in *When Knights Were Bold*, in 1949. The lady on the right is Margaret Wolfit, daughter of Sir Donald Wolfit. *Pomegranate Theatre Archive, on permanent loan to Chesterfield Local Studies Library. R Wilsher*

Figure 7. *Treasure Island,* in 1950, featuring Bernard Archard as Long John Silver. *Pomegranate Theatre Archive, on permanent loan to Chesterfield Local Studies Library, R Wilsher*

persuade the Corporation to build the theatre; they made their first appearance there less than a month after the opening.[10] Chesterfield Operatic Society had not produced a show since the year before the war had intervened, and rocketing costs were a major barrier. But a brand new venue proved a powerful stimulus; plans were soon under way for a revival of *The Gondoliers,* the society's first ever show back in 1906.[11]

The Civic's backbone, though, was the repertory company, a dedicated crew of young actors who worked hard to provide a change of programme every week. Some of those early productions have been consigned to obscurity; *The Astonished Ostrich, The Old Foolishness* and *The Indifferent Shepherd* have sunk without trace. But some titles still pop up on a regular basis: *Gaslight, An Inspector Calls, The Heiress* and *Murder at the Vicarage* can still pull the crowds.

'Rep' was acknowledged as the training ground for young actors, and many who began their careers in Chesterfield in the 1950s went on to become leading names. Peter Sallis, Harold Pinter, Margaret Tyzack and Edward Fox are all Civic 'alumni' from those earliest days (Figure 7).[12]

But despite the wealth of talent the new theatre attracted, strife and controversy rumbled beneath the surface, and on occasion threatened its very survival. In March 1950 nine members of the company, including Margaret Wolfit, Peter Sallis and manager Ian Vogler, walked out. Money lay at the heart of the theatre's problems; after an initial show of enthusiasm audiences were staying away in droves.

In the mid-1950s the repertory company was at its strongest. In 1954s pantomime David McCallum, Wilfred Brambell, Nigel Davenport and Elizabeth Spriggs all appeared on stage at the same time[13] (Figure 8). But the £5,000 raised in 1948 to cover running costs and ensure Arts Council support had now run out.

In April 1954 a public appeal was launched to secure the theatre's future. Over £2,000 was raised from local businesses on the first day, and the required £5,000 was soon in the bank. But by July it was clear that the year's losses would be heavy, and closure threatened.

Television was the factor no-one had taken into account back in the 1940s. Immediately after the war it was a novelty; a few years later it had become a growth industry. Now, unless audiences could be

Figure 8. *Aladdin*, 1954. On stage are David McCallum, Wilfred Brambell, Nigel Davenport and Elizabeth Lyon (later Sprigg), far right. *Pomegranate Theatre Archive, on permanent loan to Chesterfield Local Studies Library, R Wilsher*

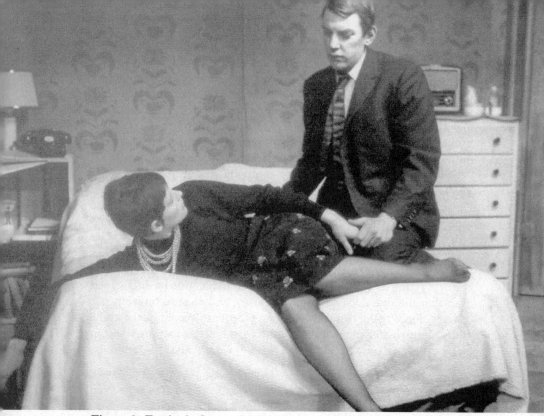

Figure 9. *Two for the Seesaw*, April 1962. A young Donald Sutherland shares an intimate scene with Jackie Burroughs. *Pomegranate Theatre Archive, on permanent loan to Chesterfield Local Studies Library, R Wilsher*

Figure 10. Donald Sutherland makes another appearance in *Anniversary Waltz*. *Pomegranate Theatre Archive, on permanent loan to Chesterfield Local Studies Library, R Wilsher*

tempted away from their sets, it appeared that live theatre's days were numbered. (Later the same year came the first suggestion that television was killing the novel as well as live theatre – but this cultural 'weed' is less powerful than it appeared; almost half a century later Chesterfield still has a theatre and all three media seem to be thriving).

Chesterfield Operatic Society has rarely had difficulty filling a theatre, and their jubilee production of *The Mikado* in March 1955 briefly enticed audiences back to the Civic. This lavish affair, with production costs topping £800, was a revival of the same show that was the society's first-ever venture in 1905 – which had cost a mere £120. But just a year later the future of the theatre was the summer's most contentious topic at Council meetings. After heated debate the Borough Council agreed to keep it alive with a grant of £12,400 over five years. (Figures 9 & 10).

And so it continued. The next major funding crisis was in 1976; in the intervening years the theatre weathered several storms, and continued to provide a training ground for young actors who went on to make their names: Betty Alberge and Ivan Beavis, for instance, both of whom later joined the cast of an innovative, unexpectedly popular new twice-weekly drama series pioneered by Granada Television. They are long gone, but *Coronation Street* thrives.

A few highlights from those years:

• In February 1958, following the tragic air crash in Munich in which seven members of the young, talented Manchester United team died, the theatre hastily rescheduled the following week's play, *Shooting Star*, which was about a young footballer.

• In 1959 there were two new arrivals: a young actress called Penelope Keith, and a new technical director called Colin McIntyre.

• In February 1961 the repertory company accepted an invitation to appear on the small screen. A recording of their production of the Philip King farce *As Black as She's Painted* formed part of ABC's Sunday afternoon Comedy Matinée series.[14]

• In January 1969 a production of Shakespeare's *Macbeth*, said by theatre people to carry a jinx, lived up to its reputation. Jack Flynn and Chris Winnera, playing Macbeth and Macduff, were both in stitches by the end of the run – literally. On Tuesday Jack was rushed to hospital after a sword fight, pouring blood from a gash above his left eyebrow; on Friday the same scene resulted in a cut hand for Chris. The theatre manager didn't think to ask if there was a doctor in the house; in fact there were four.[15]

• 1970 was Chesterfield Football Club's best season for years. Their promotion to Division Three of the Football League was marked by local musician John Madin with a specially composed march entitled *Cestrefeldia*. The Civic Theatre was the venue for its premiere at a Grand Musical Evening on 3 June, played by the Chesterfield and District Band.[16]

1976 was a turning point for the Civic Theatre. High inflation meant running costs had not been met for several years, and there was a deficit of £60,000. At the beginning of June the Arts Council announced a change in its funding policy; they were willing to provide more than half that sum – but only if there was more financial input from the local authorities whose area the theatre served. By now Chesterfield Borough Council was already contributing an annual grant of £4,000, but Derbyshire County Council and North-East Derbyshire District Council provided less than £2,000 between them. Not for the first time, the theatre's future looked precarious.

But again it survived the crisis, and limped along for another five years, to the great relief of the town's highly talented amateur groups, for whom the early 1980s proved a golden time. In 1981 Limited Company, a young and vibrant group masterminded by Tupton Hall School's drama teacher Reg Shore, mounted a striking production of *Maria Marten: Murder in the Red Barn* at the annual one-act play festival, and went on to take first prize at the National Drama Festival in Felixstowe and attract excited attention at the Edinburgh Festival Fringe.

The same summer, Chesterfield Gilbert and Sullivan Society staged its first ever full-scale stage production, *The Mikado*, playing to near-capacity houses – but when their second production was in progress a year later things were very different at the theatre.

Continuing financial difficulties forced the Borough Council into a major restructuring plan. Repertory was a dying form, and maintaining a resident company at the theatre was expensive; at the end of the 1981 season the 'rep' was disbanded, and the theatre underwent a facelift and relaunch. It would now be called the Pomegranate – a reference to part of the town crest – and would operate as a touring house, staging productions by a range of travelling companies.

The first of these, the Christmas premiere of *Rock Star*, a musical devised by new production manager David Kibart (formerly designer for the rep company), proved highly successful – yet a few months later another financial crisis loomed. But Chesterfield Gilbert and Sullivan Society's production of *The Gondoliers*, scheduled for June 1982, was moved to October to make way for *Anyone for Denis*, a popular political satire which played to packed houses – and yet again disaster was narrowly averted.

The theatre clearly led a charmed life – though when its fortunes struck an all-time low at the beginning of 1983 few would have thought so. The cancellation of two shows in succession and a deficit of over £200,000 led to a breakdown in manager David Kibart's health; his abrupt departure after less than two years at the helm was swiftly followed by the return of former theatre manager Derek Coleman. His appointment was on a month-by-month basis to help out his former employers and allow the theatre's management board to consider the long-term future – but Derek finally retired in 1995.

His twelve years at the helm were not without their memorable moments.

• The miners' strike brought Coronation Street star Pat Phoenix out in support. She visited the theatre in July 1984 – but she proved elusive, and *Derbyshire Times* feature writer Tony Cragg never did get the interview she promised.

• In May 1987 Chesterfield acquired its first purpose-built concert venue, when the new Winding Wheel opened on the site of the former Odeon cinema, converted at a cost of £1 million. It now provides facilities for dancing, meetings and private functions as well as a 1,000-seat concert hall.[17]

• 1988 was the 300th anniversary of the Glorious Revolution, a plot hatched in Chesterfield to overthrow the unpopular king, James II and instal William of Orange on the throne. Local teacher Pete Bunten commemorated the occasion with a play, *Men of Letters*; its premiere at Revolution House attracted attention from the national press, and the audience included the Prince of Wales and Chesterfield MP Tony Benn. The play, presented by award-winning theatre group Limited Company, moved to the Pomegranate from 21-25 June, and subsequently toured to London, Edinburgh, Exeter and Amsterdam.[18]

• The Pomegranate's stage is not large enough to accommodate many big-name, high-profile productions, but over the past fifteen years or so it has played host to many familiar faces from television soap and sitcom. Bonnie Langford, Robert Powell, Hannah Gordon and members of the cast of *The Archers* stand out – and who can forget Kristian Schmidt the *Neighbours* heart-throb, whose appearance in a dark thriller attracted full houses of teenage girl fans, many of whom hardly realised they were watching a play?

In 1993 the theatre underwent a major refurbishment after playing to forty-four per cent of capacity over the season: one of its most successful ever. Further improvements have taken place at intervals ever since – but it still retains its unique character. Since Derek Coleman's final goodbye there have been two managers, both young and enthusiastic, with forward-looking ideas on programming.

Live theatre, of course, requires a building to call home – but to a far greater extent it relies on a dedicated body of people for whom acting out other people's stories is a way of life. For most, especially since the demise of the repertory companies, making even a scant living at their profession requires resourcefulness and enterprise. Fame and fortune comes to only a small proportion – though North Derbyshire is not without its stars. John Hurt, for instance, was born in Shirebrook Vicarage, the son of the local parish priest.

For other, less celebrated but equally talented young thespians, low property prices and access to easy travel has made Chesterfield something of a Mecca. A community of professional actors has formed, and over the past ten years several small, adventurous companies have sprung up. Colin McIntyre, formerly technical director and later company manager at the then Civic, still mounts an annual thriller season at nearby Nottingham, and his productions tour smaller venues countrywide. So do Tabs Productions, who are gaining a national reputation for vibrant, imaginative work on a small budget. Rumpus Theatre Company's seasons at the Pomegranate invariably include more challenging plays than the popular fare of farces and thrillers: dark two-handed studio pieces and some of

Figure 11. Pomegranate Theatre, 2002. *Dennis Middleton*

Pinter's most obscure work have featured recently.

As the twenty-first century gets into its stride, amateur theatre too is thriving. Hasland Theatre Company celebrated its fiftieth anniversary in 1997, and continues to play to full houses. Chesterfield Playgoers are still going strong after almost seventy years. Eckington, Bolsover and Tupton are just a few of the areas with flourishing groups. Musicals are in the safe hands of Chesterfield Operatics, the Gilbert and Sullivan Society and a number of younger groups such as Gateway and Spotlight.

And the future is assured; youth groups like Directions Theatre Arts and Young Inspirations make sure of that.

Chesterfield, a theatre town? Of course it is (Figure 11).

Acknowledgements

I would like to thank Mrs G M Wilsher for her kind permission to use the theatre photographs taken by her late husband, Mr R Wilsher. Thanks also to the Pomegranate Theatre, *Derbyshire Times*, and Chesterfield Local Studies Library.

Notes and References

1. T P Wood's *Almanac*, 1934 pp 69-72.
2. *Derbyshire Times*, 3 September 1904.
3. *Derbyshire Times*, 27 August 1910.
4. *Derbyshire Times*, 30 December 1911.
5. *Derbyshire Times*, 21 July 1923.
6. *Derbyshire Times*, 20 February 1932.
7. *Derbyshire Times*, 22 July 1955.
8. *Derbyshire Times*, 14 December 1984.
9. *Derbyshire Times*, 25 February 1949.
10. *Derbyshire Times*, 7 April 1950.
11. *Derbyshire Times*, 31 March 1950.
12. List of Actors at Pomegranate Theatre, 1949-, Chesterfield Local Studies Library.
13. *Ibid.*
14. *Derbyshire Times*, 3 February 1961.
15. *Derbyshire Times*, 31 January 1969.
16. *Derbyshire Times*, 3 January 1970.
17. Hornsey, Brian. *Ninety Years of Cinema in Chesterfield*, 1992 p.14.
18. *Derbyshire Times*, 24 June 1988.

11. A Hundred Years in the Making: A Century of Engineering at Markham & Co Ltd

by Peter Hawkins

IN 1872 THE HARDWICK COLLIERY COMPANY placed an order with the Victoria Foundry, run by William Oliver, for the construction of two large winding engines. Part of the order was a giant drum measuring twenty-seven feet in diameter. William Oliver had run a successful operation from the 1850s onwards, at first in partnership with his father John, and after the latter's death in 1862 as sole owner, from the Victoria Foundry premises at what was formerly Shepley's Yard. He employed a hundred men and secured regular work from such prestigious clients as the Sheepbridge Coal & Iron Company among others, but the scale of the Hardwick order was greater than anything he had faced before. It soon became clear that the huge drum could not be manufactured at the Victoria Foundry, and as a result Oliver relocated to a greenfield site at Broad Oaks Meadows on the south-eastern edge of Chesterfield, bounded by the River Rother. This move, and the subsequent establishment of the Broad Oaks Foundry, mark the beginnings of what later became Markham & Co Ltd (Figures 1 & 2).

Having fulfilled the order to Hardwick, and a similar request from the Grassmoor Colliery Company in 1874, Oliver developed the site, installing new plant and straightening the course of the adjoining river. With plenty of room for expansion and easy rail access to the Midland Railway station success seemed assured, but in 1885 a slump in the coal and iron trades, coupled with massive overheads on the new factory and equipment, fatally undermined the firm. The following year William Oliver had to call in the receivers, and in 1889 the foundry was sold to industrialist Charles Paxton Markham. As Markham & Co Ltd, under its new director and his successors, it was to enjoy an unbroken run of production which would last for more than a century, and make Markham a byword for quality engineering (Figure 3).

A strong, charismatic figure, C P Markham took an active part in Chesterfield's public life, serving as a councillor for the extended borough from 1893, and three times as Mayor of Chesterfield. He

Figure 1. William Oliver at Broad Oaks Foundry, 1889. *Author's Collection*

Figure 2. Victoria Foundry, view from Saltergate, 1970s. *Author's Collection*

Figure 3. Broad Oaks Works in 1889. *Author's Collection*

was a prime mover in the demolition of the town's worst slums, contributing £10,000 for the purpose, and the newly laid Markham Road was named in his honour. More significantly for his new enterprise, he was a leading figure in the Staveley Coal & Iron Company, Parkgate Iron & Steel Co, and numerous other industrial concerns, through which he was able to ensure regular orders for the Broad Oaks Foundry. C P Markham expanded the works and had new buildings erected, while the number of his employees was increased several times over. He built houses for his workers on Picadilly Road on the far side of the Rother, close to the factory, and under his supervision Markham & Co flourished as never before, becoming one of Chesterfield's main manufacturing employers. At its peak, prior to the Second World War, a thousand men worked for the company.

Markham's primary customers were the large number of collieries in Derbyshire, Nottinghamshire and South Yorkshire, that created much of the wealth of their respective counties. For these clients the firm constructed winding and haulage gear on a massive scale. It was C P M's proud boast that one-fifth of all British coal was brought to the surface by Markham winders, and there seems little reason to doubt his claim. Nor was the success of his winding machinery confined to England. Thanks to a shrewd commercial agent, contacts were made in South Africa which resulted in the production of twenty winders for use in the gold mines during the period 1927-37, which meant regular work for many at a time of economic depression. By 1948 the company had supplied over two hundred steam and electric winding machines for home and export use, including an immense drum for South Africa which had a diameter of thirty-four feet, far outstripping the twenty-seven foot drum which had caused William Oliver to look for new premises. After the winders, tunnelling machinery was the company's other mainstay, some of it for colliery work but often for other specific projects. Again, these were usually ambitious, large-scale works of a piece with C P Markham's grandiose visions. Early in the twentieth century Markham built and supplied tunnelling equipment for the construction of London's Underground, the Mersey Tunnel, and during the 1930s in the Moscow Underground. Post-war productions would include tunnelling shields for the Dartford Tunnel under the River Thames (Figure 4).

C P Markham died in 1926. In the year prior to his death he had

Figure 4. Small excavator shield for use in London Underground. Thirty such shields were delivered within twelve weeks for this project. *Courtesy of Kvaerner Markham*

reconstituted his firm as part of the Staveley Coal & Iron Company, thus ensuring its future. Shortly afterwards, in 1928, a further important alliance was made between Markham and Bovings, water turbine designers, of London. The new agreement gave Markham a licence to build water turbines to Bovings designs, and added another lucrative string to their bow (Figures 5-6).

Part of the arrangement was the appointment of Bovings' chief Inspector, Frank Williams, as the new works manager at Broad Oaks. Williams, as significant in his way as C P Markham, is remembered as a character by several long-serving Markham employees. Always smartly dressed, he never ventured out of his office without his bowler hat, and was known as a severe taskmaster. Nothing escaped his scrutiny, and the sight of a workmate slapping the top of his head was a warning signal that the bowler and its owner had arrived, and

Figure 5. Conical drum, Order No. 7784 for Oakdale South Pit, in turbine shop, *c*.1945. To the right is a turbine for Karapiro, New Zealand, developing 42,000 hp. *Courtesy of Kvaerner Markham*

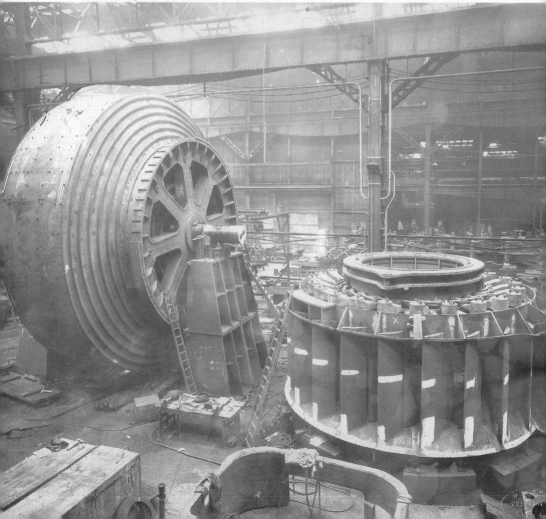

Figure 6. Looking south in Erection Shop. Compound steam winder 24-25 bore, 60 stroke, for Dallafontein Mine, South Africa, 1930s. *Courtesy of Kvaerner Markham*

that everyone had better be on the alert. On one occasion the bowler found its way into the office waste-basket and was thrown out, but once Mr Williams discovered its loss he made sure it was recovered![1] George Ison is one who remembers Mr Williams well. George was born at Doe Lea, and his father worked at Glapwell Colliery, but was determined his son would not follow him there. Markham had made the winders at Glapwell, and had a good reputation, and George signed with the company at the age of fifteen. That was June 1939, and George was to work for Markham for fifty years and a fortnight, finally retiring in July 1989. He saw both sides of his boss, as an instinctive cost-cutter, but ready to reward hard work and capable of occasional generosity. He tried to reduce George's expenses on one outside job by trying to find him cheaper digs, vainly as it proved. On the other hand, when George worked overtime installing the winding engine at Arkwright Colliery to earn extra money for his forthcoming wedding, the manager made sure he received an additional payment as a wedding present. In George's opinion, Mr Williams was a key figure in securing most of the orders for construction of water turbines, a major factor in Markham success after the Second World War.[2] By 1937 the firm had changed ownership again, Staveley selling out to John Brown & Co, Ltd, but the works continued operations as before.

With the outbreak of war in 1939, the workers at Broad Oaks found themselves involved in a series of different, but equally varied tasks. George Ison remembers some of them:

We turned out torpedo tubes for King George V class destroyers, corvette

Figure 7. 350 ton light alloy extrusion press for aircraft industry, 'Russian press', 1943. Twelve of these were completed in thirteen months for wartime use. *Courtesy of Kvaerner Markham*

machines, submarine detecting gear, landing craft, X-craft midget submarines, twelve 2500-3000 ton aluminium extrusion presses... I worked on the midget subs from the start. The work was done mostly in the small fitting shop, then moved on to the closed shop. I remember the first one was scheduled to go through by rail to Scotland. It came off the railway lines at the factory and we were running around, sweating to get jacks and so on, to get it back on track (Figure 7). [3]

Perhaps the biggest single wartime operation was the construction of the blackout building to cover the furnaces and coke ovens at Staveley Works, screening off the light that might betray them to German bombers. The construction measured 718 feet in length, stood 42 feet high and weighed a total 1,760 tons of steelwork. It was built in two spans, the first of 89 feet which surrounded the blast furnaces, the other of 57 feet shielding the pig iron beds. It was fitted successfully on the site without a day's production being lost at the blast furnaces. After the war, water turbine production came into its own as hydro-electric power became a popular option. Markham, whose workers built all three makes of turbine – Pelton, Francis and Kaplan – helped to install many of these in countries throughout the world. Not that this was by any means the sum total of its operation; in 1948 the varied work carried out at Broad Oaks included haulage gears, rolling mills and equipment, steel girders, large steel-framed buildings, light alloy extrusion presses, spun cast iron plant, blast furnace plant, large iron castings and research equipment in addition to the turbine and tunnelling operations.

The firm's reputation for quality, and its reliability as a regular employer drew a loyal response from its workforce, several of whom served the company for many years. A close associate of George Ison was Eddie Lawrence, whose father worked fifty-one years for Markham, and who himself put in forty-nine years, joining at fourteen in 1943 and retiring in 1992. ('I thought we'd do the hundred years between us, and he could do the odd one.').[4] Signed on by Mr Williams, he started work on the fettling heap, removing sand from the cores of the large metal castings, 'a filthy job – you ended up looking as if you'd been down the pit.'[5] He went on to work with George on Kaplan water turbines for Mankala (Finland), Piakowski (Poland), Owen Falls (Uganda) and the Kariba Dam in Africa, and on colliery equipment breakdown and maintenance work, before moving on to the Drawing Office where the main contracts were for National Coal Board winding engines. On another occasion George found himself working for the Admiralty at Haslar on behalf of the firm, putting together the Portsmouth water cavitation tunnel, where model ships were tested in a huge tank half a mile in length. Colin Burton, whose father had been a night-watchman for Markham, joined at fifteen in 1951 and worked there for forty-seven years before retirement in 1998. He and his family lived in the company's houses on Picadilly Road, and he comments that, although pay wasn't that good, there was always plenty of overtime, and the rents were modest. Picadilly Road's electricity was supplied by a unique 30-cycle system which required a special transformer to obtain a television signal! Like most of his colleagues, he enjoyed his time with Markham, recalling 'most people where we lived never thought of working for anyone else.'[6] Appointed foreman at twenty-nine, he helped produce colliery winders, turbines and aluminium surface torpedo tubes in the heavy engineering section.

Dennis Goodhind, who joined Markham at fifteen, and whose long stay with the firm (1946-93) was only briefly interrupted by National Service, was office boy in the company Rates Office before moving on to the machine shop and after 1953 worked as a draughtsman. Dennis also encountered Mr Williams, and remembers another aspect of his character, namely his keen interest in sport. The Broad Oaks site had its own football ground, cricket pitch, bowling green and tennis courts, and apparently Mr Williams was always on the lookout for former or potential footballers and cricketers.If you could play, you were in with the chance of a job, and at one time there were so many ex-professional soccer players on the strength that Dennis feels: 'We had a team good enough to beat Chesterfield.'[7] There are others who remember the time in the terrible winter of 1947, when at the height of a fuel shortage Mr Williams had braziers set out around the frozen Markham football pitch to thaw it out in order for a big match to go ahead!

What didn't the men at Markham make in those days? Winding engines were sent to Rose Deep in Australia, complete with a new braking system designed in-house. Alan Barnes, with the firm from the age of fourteen on a spell of duty that ran 1946-93, began like most of his colleagues on the fettling heap, and later graduated to steamhammer-driving in the blacksmith's shop. Here the workers were paid for each item produced, and Alan recalls that the official record was marked by foreman Harry Brooks on a slat of wood that was whitewashed over at the end of each day! In spite of these seemingly primitive methods, the shop turned out work to Markham's usual precise standards. Later on Alan worked on folding

Figure 8. Water turbines awaiting delivery to Scotland, 1930s. *Courtesy of Kvaerner Markham*

and wrapping machines used for aerofoil sections in aircraft production, and afterwards tested colliery haulers. He also remembers the stowage equipment that proved a useful earner for Markhams.[8] The idea, borrowed from Germany, was to fill in the seam behind the excavated coal by forcing the waste in by machines using compressed air. It worked well, but after several years the NCB decided the method was too expensive and left the shafts unfilled, preferring to pay the subsidence costs (Figures 8-9).

Figure 9. Earlier housing on Picadilly Road, built by C P Markham for his workers, April 2002. *Dennis Middleton*

Markham also built the refuelling machine for the AGR (Advanced Gas-Cooled Reactor) at Windscale. Dennis Goodhind, who took part in the operation, recalls it as:

> *operating inside a building like a large football. Trucks running up and down and crashing sideways allowed the machine to service the 365 positions on the reactor floor with the fuel elements. The machine could be revolved into position, then a grab was lowered to remove the spent element, the segment was spun and a new element lowered. A television camera could be lowered into the reactor if any problem arose due to broken elements.*[9]

Then there was the huge six hundred ton road deck Markham built as a substitute roadway to keep the traffic running while the Jubilee Line of the London Underground line was being extended. The massive creation had a trial run in the yard at Broad Oaks, and the itemised and colour-coded parts were shipped to London. 'It was like a military operation', Dennis Goodhind remembers:

> *The deck was in the middle of Oxford Street, with four road junctions. It had pedestrian walkways which had to be level – all the roads were different levels and curvatures, and there was a pub at the end of one. You didn't want them coming out on a slope!*[10]

By the 1960s the market had begun to contract. The wholesale installation of electric winders effectively killed the production of steam winders at Broad Oaks, and many Third World countries could no longer afford to install hydro-electric schemes.

Markhams enjoyed something of an Indian summer in the 1970s when the government's Plan for Coal resulted in a major order of winders from the firm by the NCB. The nationwide overhaul of colliery braking systems that followed the Markham Colliery tragedy of 1973 also brought in work, but within a few years these orders disappeared. The firm remained heavily reliant on water turbine work, for both foreign and domestic use. The turbines supplied to Dinorwic in Wales, were one example that resulted in a useful profit. Later on, in the 1980s, the company would manufacture four bulb turbine runners – the largest made at the time – for the prestigious Vidalia project on the Mississippi River in Lousiana. A big tunnelling contract was secured for the drainage system in Mexico City in 1967. It had to be done at top speed, as Eddie Lawrence recalls:

We had twelve months to produce three machines from the drawings to the finished product, and ship them off – a hell of a job![11]

The three Universal soft-ground slurry-type tunnelling machines were duly supplied on time, but sadly, did not prove to be very profitable.

In 1986 John Brown & Co Ltd became part of the Trafalgar House Group, but this situation did not last for long. By 1996 Trafalgar House were bought out by the Norweigan group Kvaerner Brug, and the water turbine work that had been Markham's post-war mainstay was transferred to Norway. The Markham workforce concentrated once more on tunnelling machines and shields. In 1984 they made a full-face hard-rock tunnelling machine which was capable of boring through granite, for use in Lodigiani, Italy. A few years later, in 1987, they secured a contract worth £15 million when in partnership with rock tunnelling specialists Robbins of America they constructed two full-face tunnel boring machines for the driving of the Channel Tunnel from the English side. One of the most prestigious projects ever undertaken by the firm, it involved the construction of two monstrous tunnelling machines, each measuring two hundred and twenty metres in length and weighing 1300 tonnes. Fitted with tungsten-tipped picks, the machines were capable of cutting a tunnel 8.36 metres in diameter and installing behind them a segmented concrete lining 0.38 metres thick. It was a superb achievement, but unfortunately came too late to save the company. As markets dwindled, the workforce was cut , the eight hundred and fifty workers of the 1960s rapidly reduced to four hundred, and eventually to half that. The men of Markham went out on a high

Figure 10. Shepherd Homes' new Riverside Village on the former Markham factory site, Picadilly Road, April 2002. *Dennis Middleton*

note. Their final job, a tunnelling shield for Manapouri hydro-electric scheme in New Zealand, was the largest they had ever made, bigger even than the huge Channel Tunnel machines.

In 1998 the Broad Oaks works was closed, some of the workforce transferred to the former Davy United site, now Kvaerner Metals, in

Figure 11. Markham office building on Hollis Lane, the View from Clayton Street, April 2002. *Dennis Middleton*

Sheffield. Colin Burton, who retired that year, was one of the last to leave. It was a sad day for him, as it was for many of his long-serving colleagues. For most veteran workers at Markham, the pay had never been high. George Ison remembers he started on the fettling heap at 13s 1d (65p) and as an apprentice fitter saw his pay reduced to 10s 8d (53p),[12] and much later on Alan Barnes recalls that the base fitting rate stayed for years at 66s (£3-30p),[13] but then again it does not seem to have been a key consideration. Regular employment for a firm with a reputation for quality , the opportunity for overtime, and the comradeship of their fellows, appear to have been every bit as important to them.

Today, the Markham site has all but vanished, the factory buildings demolished and replaced by Shepherd Homes' Riverside Village housing estate (Figure 10). Only the old office building, fronting on to Hollis Lane, still survives (Figure 11). But memories of those earlier days do not die so easily. From the time Markham & Co, Ltd took its name from its new owner C P Markham in 1889, to final closure in 1998, the firm grew and flourished for a hundred and nine years. During that time it established itself as a leader in precision engineering, carrying out a staggering variety of operations in wartime and peacetime alike, and ensuring its fame spread far beyond Chesterfield across the world. The men of Markham helped to make that name, investing their effort and skills and most of their working lives in the success of the firm. Hopefully, this article is a tribute to the scale of their achievement.

Acknowledgements

I would like to express my grateful thanks to George Ison, Eddie Lawrence, Alan Barnes, Colin Burton and Dennis Goodhind, my former work colleagues at Markham & Co, Ltd, for taking the time to share their memories of the company and its history, and for the loan of photographs to illustrate this article.

Notes and References

1. Dennis Goodhind, taped interview 27 March 2002.
2. George Ison, taped interview 27 March 2002.
3. *Ibid.*
4. Eddie Lawrence, taped interview 27 March 2002.
5. *Ibid.*
6. Colin Burton, taped interview 27 March 2002.
7. Dennis Goodhind, taped interview 27 March 2002.
8. Alan Barnes, taped interview 27 March 2002.
9. Dennis Goodhind, taped interview 27 March 2002.
10. *Ibid.*
11. Eddie Lawrence, taped interview 27 March 2002.
12. George Ison, taped interview 27 March 2002.
13. Alan Barnes, taped interview 27 March 2002.

12. CELEBRATED CONFECTIONS AND MONSTER CAKES

by Brian Austin

IT IS NOT GENERALLY APPRECIATED that, for centuries, Chesterfield has been a centre of excellence for cake-making, confectionery, cookery and tasty sauces. In this year of 2002 these are still areas of commercial, craft and industrial significance, although frequently overlooked by promoters of the town's image. A notable modern example is Jackson's the Bakers on Low Pavement, who, besides making celebration cakes and other fine confectionery for discerning customers, also baked a huge 'Mr Blobby' cake for television celebrity Noel Edmonds in the not too distant past.[1] Another famous firm known throughout the world is Cadbury Trebor Bassett who makes mints, jelly babies and other sweets at their plant on Brimington Road. Chesterfield is still a 'Centre of Innovative and Creative Confectionery' whose origins date back to Roman times.

Throughout its history the town of Chesterfield has been promoted under a variety of titles. Each of these has highlighted some important aspect of its character. In medieval days it was designated the capital of the Scarsdale Hundred, since it was the major borough of North Derbyshire and administrative centre for the rich Vale of Scarsdale. This fertile area, with its mineral wealth, stretched southwards from the River Sheaf in Sheffield, South Yorkshire, down to Alfreton in the middle of Derbyshire. With the onset of the Industrial Revolution and the coming of the railways, which led to a considerable expansion of local coal, iron, chemical and engineering industries, Chesterfield's aldermen and councillors proclaimed their town to be a major industrial centre. So, fifty years ago, visitors to the town could not help but notice large and prominent signs, sited on the verges of the main entrance roads which announced they were approaching 'CHESTERFIELD – The Centre of Industrial England.' However, with the contraction and decline of these heavy industries, and the need for the borough to establish a new marketing identity, modern governing fathers have decided to reinvent Chesterfield in its earlier medieval image, advertising it as an 'Historic Market Town', no hint of mints, confectionery and cakes.

This hill-top settlement started as a centre of control and

communication, meetings and markets when the conquering Roman legions built their fort here. These military imperialists also breathed new life into Scarsdale when they constructed a network of roads which converged on the fort itself. New roads and new people enabled new ideas, new methods, and most importantly, new tastes to become a part of Chesterfield life. Since the Roman soldiers and citizens loved their sausages, spices and sweetmeats, they established a tradition for fine food which continued to develop through the following centuries.

In the eighteenth century, after the ravages of the Civil War, the upheaval of the 'Glorious Revolution', the founding of Chesterfield Races and the building of the Chesterfield Canal, the town and its market square developed as places of prosperity, pleasure and entertainment. Aristocrats and gentlemen of means converged on Chesterfield and Scarsdale, and several set up homes in and around the town. Local ladies were often seen as suitable wives and mothers for 'blue-blooded' husbands and children, and so they married into the aristocratic Irish, Scottish and French families – the Butlers, Murrays and D'Henins. The landed gentry, including the Bright family from nearby Hallamshire and the Jebbs from Nottingham and Mansfield, also selected local brides with valuable land and substantial dowries.[2] All these wealthy locals and discerning Georgians demanded the best of food in their homes and hostelries, and so the centre of the small borough of Chesterfield produced inns, shops and cooks of distinction to satisfy this demand. The inns and shops were centred around the Market Place, with the *Castle* (later the *Angel*) hotel at the top of the sloping market square and the confectioners and cooks at the bottom, along Low and Central Pavement (Figure 1).

Figure 1. Map of Chesterfield town centre showing sites of celebrity bakers and confectioners. *Brian Austin Collection*

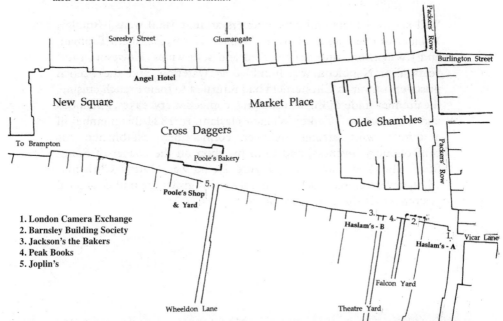

The *Angel* – not to be confused with the *Old Angel*, on Packers' Row, had under its previous name *The Castle,* become accepted as the premier hostelry and coaching inn for the town, and the owners regularly provided lunches and dinners for affluent, Georgian gourmet diners who attended Race Balls and Literary and Debating Society Dinners. The Society for the Prosecution of Felons, which two hundred years ago had over a hundred property-owning members from all over the Scarsdale area, also held dinners and meetings there on many occasions. All these sophisticated customers expected, and were served, the best of food.[3]

Around 1780 the need for cookery courses was satisfied by Sarah Sims, this Georgian Delia Smith, who used her father's premises as a training centre, and the *Derby Mercury* for advertising:

SARAH SIMS

INTENDS *opening her PASTRY SCHOOL,*
On MONDAY, November 12, 1781, at her Father's, F
SIMS, near the Market-Place, CHESTERFIELD. All thofe
who pleafe to favor her with their Children, may depend on the
utmoft care being taken for their beft Inftruction.
Alfo begs leave to return her moft fincere Thanks for the
Very great Encouragement fhe has already met with, and
Hopes for the Continuance of their Favours; and for the fu-
ture, purpofes beginning her School fix Weeks before Chrift-
mas-Day, by
Their most obedient humble Servant,

SARAH SIMS

+ She likewife bones Fifh and Fowl.
N.B. Children out of the Country may have Lodgings at
the fame Place.[4]

Well-known bakers and confectioners around 1800 were J Bradley, William Bradley, Joseph Cooper, William Hardy, Elizabeth Tupman, and J Wilkinson, who also stocked and sold wines. However, a few years after Napoleon was humbled at Waterloo, and the French prisoners of war in Chesterfield had returned to their French cuisine, the premier trade in English cooking, confectionery, cakes, fine foods and wines was satisfied by William Haslam. In 1824 this member of a family with strong Ashover connections established his confectionery business, and from his shop on the corner of South Street and Low Pavement[5] (Figure 2), he was, during Christmas 1829, advertising and sending thanks to his growing number of local customers via the *Derbyshire Courier:*

Figure 2. Present day site of William Haslam's shop, Low Pavement.
Brian Austin Collection

WILLIAM HASLAM
CONFECTIONER, & c
SOUTH STREET, CHESTERFIELD

BEGS *leave most respectfully to return his grateful ac-*
Knowledgements to his numerous Friends, and the Pub-
Lic of Chesterfield and its neighbourhood, for their very
Liberal support since his commencement in Business; and
Begs leave to inform them that in addition to the above
Business, he has commenced Selling

BRITISH WINES
Of the best quality, and on the most reasonable terms; he

Figure 3. Haslam's Twelfth Night Cakes. *Author's drawing, based on Cruikshank. Brian Austin Collection*

> *Likewise desires to inform them, that previous to the 6th of*
> *January, (Twelfth Night) he will have on hand a quantity*
> *Of* **ORNAMENTED CAKES** *of all sizes; and, as usual, will*
> *Decorate his Shop on the above night; and will be much*
> *Obliged by any friends favouring him with a call, -- and begs*
> *To assure them that no exertions on his part shall be wanting.*[6]

William's fine food and Twelfth Night Cakes became very popular indeed, and were much in demand. The scenes at Haslam's shop (Figure 3) were described by a local commentator in the *Derbyshire Chronicle* of 11 January:

> **TWELFTH NIGHT** – *On Monday night the shop of Mr*
> *Haslam, confectioner & c, Chesterfield, was a scene of great*

attraction. The interior of the shop was tastefully decorated and a variety of entertaining objects were skilfully arranged, over which a pleasing lustre was shed by a number of variegated lamps.

Every available place was occupied with rich cakes of various sizes,with their attractive and inviting icing, and coloured ornaments.

Many glistening eyes were cast upon the delicious objects displayed to the admiring gaze of hundreds, and we doubt not that in the lottery that followed that many were disappointed in their expectations, and others made glad.

We hope that Mr Haslam is amply remunerated for his trouble.[7]

To meet the growing demand for his fine confectionery, William Haslam took on apprentices, one of whom was young George Bassett from Ashover. The Bassett family seemed keen on careers in cakes and confectionery, since George's brother William was also apprenticed to another Chesterfield grocer, William Bingham, who had a business at the junction of Vicar Lane and Lordsmill Street.[8] At that time, William Haslam's son, Charles, was only two or three years old, but no doubt he was also destined to enter the family cake and confectionery business, like his older brother John, who was also apprenticed to their father.[9] But it was to be young Charles who would achieve fame by innovating and improving the range of fine food, wines and sauces, and his cooking and commercial acumen would eventually win him Royal recognition in 1857.

When the founding father of the firm died during the Christmas period of 1849, Charles and his sister took control of the business. Charles promoted and advertised Haslam's cakes, biscuits, fruits, wines and, most importantly, the special 'Chesterfield sauce'. This sauce, created to accompany and enhance the flavour of fish and meat, received favourable comment from both customers and the local press. In the spring of 1854, the *Derbyshire Courier* hailed it as superior to the renowned Harvey's Sauce made in Portman Square, London. The paper's culinary connoisseur claimed the 'Chesterfield Sauce' to be 'less fluid than the famed Harvey's Sauce, equal to it in flavour, while it is superior in imparting a warmth and tone to the palate.'[10]

Encouraged by this customer reaction, former apprentice George Bassett who had moved to his own premises in Fargate sold the same from Sheffield,[11] and no doubt by fellow members of the ancient Chesterfield Bowling Club, Charles determined to send a sample of his merchandise

Figure 4. Sauce Maker to the Queen! *Brian Austin Collection*

"Are you Saucemaker to the Queen?"
"Indeed I am, Sir." *Brian Austin Collection*

to Queen Victoria. His confidence in the quality of his sauce was rewarded when, in the summer of 1857, he was officially informed that Her Majesty was not merely amused but delighted with 'Chesterfield Sauce'. From that point onwards, the Haslam kitchen on Low Pavement became 'The Royal Sauce Manufactory' and the regal coat of arms crowned the name of Charles Haslam. Delighted himself, Charles was not at all reticent in announcing himself as 'Sauce maker to the Queen'! (Figure 4)

When Charles Haslam died, the family business eventually passed into the capable hands of T B Milner, who had worked ten years with the firm. The change of ownership did not result in the demise of Chesterfield Celebration Cakes and fine pastries, which continued to be produced at Low Pavement. Milner's maintained its inherited reputation and went on to bake bread which, in open competition, was adjudged to be 'the best in the Kingdom.'(Figure 5) So Charles Haslam

Figure 5. T B Milner (formerly Haslam's) Pastry Cook & Confectioner. *Brian A Austin Collection.*

T. B. MILNER,

(Late HASLAM,)

Pastry Cook & Confectioner,

Begs to inform his patrons and the public generally that he has erected **Two Patent Ovens** in his new and enlarged Bakery, to meet the increased requirements of his business.

A Restaurant is being fitted up.

Public Baking in the New Patent Ovens is carried on **continuously** from 7 in the morning till 6 in the evening.

WEDDINGS, BALLS, DINNERS, TEAS, &c., CATERED FOR.

British and Foreign Wines.

ARTISTIC BRIDE CAKES.

33, LOW PAVEMENT, CHESTERFIELD.

was supported by his former staff and successors in maintaining Chesterfield as a Victorian centre of eating excellence.

In the meantime, while Charles was making moves for royal recognition, another baker, John Poole, situated at the opposite end of the Market Place, also created special cakes which made the words 'Chesterfield' and 'Poole' known throughout the realm. But whereas Haslam had provided exceptional quality, John Poole specialised in record-breaking quantity with 'The Largest Lottery Cakes in the World!'

John Poole, a baker and also a butcher, originated from Mansfield in Nottinghamshire. When he set up in Chesterfield he targeted the large and growing market of industrial workers and institutions such as the Militia, from his bakery in the *Cross Daggers*. This was in contrast to Haslam, who supplied a smaller but more affluent clientele which included Frederick Swanwick, a close associate of the railway pioneer George Stephenson, who also ate well in nearby Tapton House.

> **GOOD NEWS FOR HOME**
> **WORKING MEN, READ THIS! AND JUDGE FOR**
> **YOURSELVES!!**
> **QUALITY IS THE ONLY TRUE TEST OF**
> **CHEAPNESS!**
> **ONE FOUR-POUND LOAF FOR SIX PENCE!**
> *One pound of Bacon for Six Pence!*
> **ONE POUND OF FINE-FLAVOURED CHEESE FOR**
> **SIXPENCE HALFPENNY!**
> **AT J POOLE'S OLD-ESTABLISHED PROVISION**
> **STORES,**
> **LOW PAVEMENT, CHESTERFIELD**
> **N B FRESH CLOTH BUTTER EVERY WEEK.**[12]

As mentioned previously, complimentary Twelfth Night cakes were a long-standing tradition in Victorian Chesterfield, and all the confectioners participated in producing this free festive fare. A prominent supplier, Mr Reynolds in Burlington Street, also gave customers raffle tickets when they bought his cakes, and held a prize draw. Prize-winners in January 1853 were James Newton of Cavendish Street and S Shepley of Claughton's, who won £1 1s (£1 5p) each, and Miss Ann Salt of Cutthorpe who claimed 14s 6d (72.5p).[13] However, by Christmas 1853 a combination of confectioners in the town had decided that this expensive custom of Christmas Boxes should stop, since it was reducing their profits. This decision created a marketing and commercial opportunity which John Poole, an independent entrepreneur, was quick to exploit.

He decided to continue the tradition of prizes and Christmas Cakes by cooking a large cake – not a pudding! – which had gold rings, rather than the usual 3d (1.25p) bits, mixed in with the other succulent ingredients. After all, Poole reasoned, who in Chesterfield could resist the chance to find a gold wedding ring in their slice of Christmas Eve cake, a pound of which cost only a shilling (5p). He judged human nature correctly, and his large prize cake, weighing one hundredweight (56 kilos), sold out in just two hours when it was cut on Christmas Eve. Ever the opportunist, Poole took advantage of the great demand and cooked another even larger cake – this time weighing five hundredweights (280 kilos) and holding twelve rings – which he advertised to be sold on 6 and 7 January 1854.[14]

John Poole continued to bake larger cakes in 1854 and 1855. His cake in the latter year weighed about two tons, and the lottery prizes numbered a hundred, with a total value of £63. The first prize was a silver watch made by Mr Robinson of South Street and valued at five guineas. This remarkable baker also introduced another distinctive attraction that same year, when he decorated his shop with an illuminated star, flanked on either side by the initials of the Queen and the Emperor Napoleon III. These prizes and decorations seemed appropriate for the cake which was six feet six inches (2 metres) in diameter, three feet four inches (1 metre) high, with a volume of four cubic yards. It was reported that the ingredients would fill three railway waggons, and the area covered was about fifteen square yards! Mr Reynolds, a rival baker on High Street, also joined in the monster cake-making, but his prizes and cakes were puny compared with John Poole's 'Leviathan Lottery Cake of Low Pavements'![15] Mr Reynolds's 1st Prize of a swing kettle with a stand was inferior to a silver watch, and his cake was a mere two feet four inches (less than 1 metre) high. No wonder that he envied John Poole's trade, which by now enjoyed a considerable mail order business. One of his lady customers in Yorkshire even ordered slices of Poole's cake which she used as an attraction at her lottery tea parties!

Mr Poole's monster cakes reached their peak in 1856, a year before Charles Haslam was honoured by Queen Victoria. By this time these monster cakes had become a Chesterfield institution, and famous throughout adjoining counties. They would be well known in nearby Sheffield, where the businessmen and residents were keen to promote their city as one of the premier sites in

THE CHESTERFIELD CAKE FOR 1856.
THE SIXTH ANNUAL SALE

THE extraordinary and unprecedented demand for the **CHRISTMAS CAKE** hitherto made by Mr. **JOHN POOLE**, having secured for him the confidence of the public of Chesterfield and the principal Towns in the Midland Counties, he ventures this year t o surpass his former efforts by making the Largest and Best Cake ever made in the World! which will be of the Enormous Weight of

UPWARDS OF THREE TONS !

Along with the sale of it, will be distributed (as in past sales), **107 GIFTS**, value £93 14s 0d., consisting of the following viz:-

	£	s	d
A splendid Fat Pig (alive) value	8	8	0

Fed expressly for the occasion, by Mr G Bollington, farmer, Ashover - Milltown, and may be seen in Chesterfield Cattle Market on Saturday, Dec. 20th, or previous, at the Wash Farm, Ashover.

	£	s	d
4 Patent Lever Silver Watches, value ..	16	10	0

Guaranteed by the Makers - - No. 1, Mr. Robinson, No. 2, Mrs Thompson, No. 3. Mr. Mee, No. 4. Mr. Slack.

	£	s	d
1 Handsome set of Mahogany Drawers, cicular fronts, value	5	0	0

May be seen at Mr. Shaw's , Cabinet Maker

	£	s	d
70 lbs. of Superfine Tea, at 5s.per lb. value	17	10	0
1 Bag of Superfine Flour (18 stones), value	2	10	0
30 Beautifully chased Silver-plated Tea Pots	43	10	0
107 Gifts Total Value....	£93	14	0

The recipients of Last Year's Gifts were publicly adver-tised, and a copy of the same may be had by any one en-closing a Postage Stamp with their address. The Cake will be Sold at

ONE SHILLING PER POUND ! !

To commence cutting on THURSDAY, the 18th of DE-CEMBER, and will be on view the Saturday previous, December 13th, - 18th.

N.B. - - Parties at a distance, wishing to obtain a cut of the above, are particularly requested to make early appli-cations, as last year Mr. P., was put to much inconvenience and loss, in returning orders and remittances, which did not arrive in time. Post Office Orders, &c., promptly at-tended to, if addressed to **Mr. JOHN POOLE,** Confec-tioner, Low pavement and Burlington - street, Chesterfield.

Figure 6. The Chesterfield Cake for 1856. *Derbyshire Times, December 1855*

Figure 7. Jackson's Monster Cakes in 2002. *Brian Austin Collection*

Victorian Britain. It seems highly probable that a showman of that city, Thomas Youdan, saw 'Monster Cakes' as a means of publicity. He commissioned such a cake from a confectioner in Sheffield, stipulating a delivery date of 1 January 1856, and a weight between four and five tons.

John Poole made his biggest cake – a three-tonner! – for Christmas 1856. The lottery prizes were the best ever, but he probably realised he could not compete with the much larger Sheffield confectioner. (Figure 6)

By a supreme irony, the monster cake of Sheffield was made by none other than George Bassett, former apprentice of Charles Haslam, confectioner of Low Pavement! The Chesterfield tradition of Monster Cakes is continued today by Jackson's on Low Pavement (Figure 7). The taste is great, and of course, size doesn't matter.

Notes and References

1. *Derbyshire Times*, 29 August 1996.
2. Debrett's *Peerage and Landed Gentry; Chesterfield Parish Church records 1804-14; Wingerworth Parish Church records* 1719; *Derby Mercury,* 8 September, 15 September 1758.
3. *Derby Mercury*, years 1798-.
4. *Derby Mercury*, 25 October-1 November 1781.
5. *Derbyshire Courier*, 7 January 1854.
6. *Derbyshire Courier*, 26 December 1829.
7. *Derbyshire Chronicle*, 11 January 1830.
8. *Derbyshire Courier*, 11 March 1837.
9. 1841 Chesterfield Census.
10. *Derbyshire Courier*, March 1854.
11. *Derbyshire Courier*, 7 October 1854.
12. *Derbyshire Times*, 10 November 1855.
13. *Derbyshire Courier*, 8 January 1853.
14. *Derbyshire Courier*, 31 December 1853.
15. *Derbyshire Times*, 22 December 1855.

CONTRIBUTORS

THE EDITOR
1. THOSE DANCE BAND DAYS: THE RISE AND FALL OF CHESTERFIELD'S RENDEZVOUS DANCE HALL

Geoffrey Sadler was born in Mansfield Woodhouse, Nottinghamshire in 1943. Educated at Queen Elizabeth's Grammar School for Boys in Mansfield, he worked for four years as an assistant in Mansfield Library before studying for his ALA at Manchester Library School in 1965-66. In the latter year he joined the Derbyshire Library Service and crossed the border to Shirebrook, Derbyshire, where he has remained ever since. For the past seventeen years he has worked as Assistant Librarian in the Local Studies Library at Chesterfield, and also pursued his interest in local history. Author of three photographic works on Shirebrook's past, and *Who Was Who, the Black and Whites: Shirebrook FC Players 1911-33* (2000), co-author with Antoni Snarski of *Journey to Freedom* (1900), and editor of Ralph Batteson's wartime memoir *St Nazaire to Shepperton: a Sailor's Odyssey* (1996), his *Chesterfield: History and Guide* (2001) is the first single volume history of the town to appear since the 1970s; he is also the author of twenty-eight Western novels under his pseudonyms of 'Jeff Sadler' and 'Wes Calhoun', and has edited *Twentieth Century Western Writers* (1991) for St James Press/Gale Research. Currently researching a book on Chesterfield and North Derbyshire crimes in Wharncliffe's *Foul Deeds* series, his other works in progress include a thriller, a historical novel, more Westerns, and interviews for an oral history project run by Derbyshire Library Service.

2. THE DIXONS AND WHITTINGTON GLASS HOUSE

Trevor Nurse has lived all his life in New Whittington and is the fourth native generation of his family, his great-grandfather arriving here in 1884 after twenty years of army service. His father and grandfather were both miners who worked in the many local collieries, all of which have now disappeared. Trevor left school at fifteen to begin work as a plumber, but later returned to the academic world, studying at Chesterfield College and after doing his National Service was appointed a lecturer at Rotherham College. From here he moved to Sheffield College, where he taught for twenty years. Now retired, he loves to pursue his hobby of local history, and thoroughly enjoys writing about and sketching the old buildings around his home village.

3. TRICKS OF THE TRADE

Born in Chesterfield, **David Howes** left school at fifteen to work as a hairdresser's apprentice, and regards himself as largely self-educated. Married with a son and two grandchildren, his forty-seven years as a gent's hairdresser in Chesterfield brought him into contact with several leading local tradesmen and sparked an interest in the commercial history of the town, which he has since pursued. Other interests include numismatics, crown green bowling and the collection of Chesterfield ephemera. A member of Chesterfield & District Local History Society and Chesterfield Collectors' Club, he is frequently in demand as a speaker on the town's shops and tradesmen.

4. BRAMPTON CHILDHOOD MEMORIES

A lifelong Cestrefeldian, **John Lilley** was born in Brampton where he lived until the age of twenty-five, moving to his present home in the neighbouring district of Walton. Educated at Old Road Junior School and Chesterfield Grammar School, he joined Chesterfield Public Library as an assistant, gaining his professional qualifications at the Loughborough School of Librarianship. For many years Reference Librarian at the old library premises at the Stephenson Memorial Hall, he was appointed Local Studies Librarian when the new library opened at New Beetwell Street in 1985, and served in the post until retirement in March 2000. Still remembered by colleagues for his unrivalled local knowledge and expertise, he has continued to pursue his interest in local history, with membership of two Local History and two County Family History Societies. His other interests are choral singing, supporting Chesterfield FC, and collecting First Day covers.

5. I REMEMBER ARKWRIGHT

Charles Dickens was born in 1940 in Arkwright Town, where he lived until 1963. Having left school with no academic qualifications, but a keen interest in local football, he tried his hand at several jobs, including a brief stint in the Army before returning to work as a miner at Arkwright Colliery for more than twenty years. Since 1987 he has been employed as a member of the Pavements security staff by Chesterfield Borough Council, with responsibility for Chesterfield Library. A well-known and popular local character, his literary name and place of work have earned him occasional mention in the national press. *I Remember Arkwright* is his first venture into print as an author in his own right.

---

6. GHOSTS OF CHESTERFIELD

Carol Brindle is a former Secondary School English teacher who worked in Special Needs Learning Support during the latter years of her career. She trained as a Blue Badge Tourist Guide in the winter of 1992-93; this is a nationally recognised qualification, and guides are registered with the Tourist Boards. Carol is also a member of the Institute of Tourist Guiding. Originally from Scarborough, she has become a devoted fan of beautiful Derbyshire during her eighteen years in the county. She is married to Philip, a company director, and they have two married daughters, Sheridan and Helen. Carol loves her job, giving commentaries on coaches and leading visitors on guided walks, covering twelve major towns and villages in Derbyshire. She also gives un-illustrated talks to clubs and organisations on Derbyshire topics. Carol recently chaired a National Committee for the London-based Guild of Registered Tourist guides, and is currently chair of the Derbyshire Association. Her information comes from books, magazines, original documents, personal interviews and on-site visits. Reading local newspapers and magazines also keeps her up to date. In the case of ghost stories, people are only too willing to tell of their own experiences, and this first-hand information is invaluable. Many will also add information to stories and confirm the facts.

---

7. VICTORIAN WINGERWORTH – A 'CLOSE' PARISH?

David Edwards was born in Neath and educated there and at Leeds University, from where he graduated with a BSc in Gas Engineering and a PhD for research on pulverised fuel combustion. Most of his working life was spent with the British Coke Research

Association and its successors at Wingerworth, where he was in charge of the technical information service. He has researched the history of Wingerworth for the past thirty-five years, publishing inter alia *The Hunlokes of Wingerworth Hall* (1976) and *Wingerworth Landscape: a Historical Guide* (1997). His other historical publications include editions of the *Derbyshire Hearth Tax Assessments* (1982) and of *Derbyshire P C C Wills* (1998) for Derbyshire Record Society (of which he is treasurer and assistant editor), a study of a street in Chesterfield: *The Glumangate Story* (1994) and *A Historical Gazetteer and Bibliography of By-product Coking Plants in the United Kingdom* (2001).

---

8. SPITAL THROUGH THE AGES

Sonia Preece has from Grammar School days had a lifelong love of history, both local and of the Tudor period. Now that her two sons are grown up she finds she is able to spend more time studying and researching history. She is at present attending a course at Nottingham University, and hopes next year to attain her MA in History. Her work as a National Trust volunteer also enables her to follow her love of history, and as a guide to pass on her knowledge to visitors. Sonia is particularly fascinated by Spital's history, especially the recent discovery of the medieval priest's grave.

*By kind permission of
M Dudley, Ripley*

As Secretary of the Spital Local History Group she was instrumental in organising his reburial at Spital Cemetery.

9. CHESTERFIELD RAGGED SCHOOL

David Botham is an architect with Chesterfield Borough Council. In his 'spare time' he conducts a choir based at the old chapel and acts as Secretary to the Ragged School with the help of his wife (and IT support worker) Sue. They have two grown-up children. An acknowledged expert on the school and its history, David is also a talented artist who is in regular demand as designer of the choir's annual Christmas card. He  and Sue welcome visitors to all the services at the chapel, and further details are available on the family's web site at: **www.dsbotham.freeserve.co.uk/ragged school.**

10. CHESTERFIELD: AN UNEXPECTED THEATRE TOWN

Lynne Patrick is a working writer with wide experience of freelance journalism. She is arts correspondent and main theatre critic for the *Derbyshire Times*, the county's leading weekly newspaper, and columnist for *New Writer*, a quality magazine for aspiring authors. Her personality profiles, human interest and travel features have appeared in numerous publications including the *Guardian*, the *Independent* and *Contemporary Review*. She  also tutors in creative writing, runs a small, high-quality correspondence support and appraisal service for aspiring writers, and organises one of the largest UK-based short story awards.

11. A HUNDRED YEARS IN THE MAKING: A CENTURY OF ENGINEERING AT MARKHAM & CO. LIMITED

Peter Hawkins was born in Sheffield in 1937, and educated at Wiseman Secondary Modern School. Leaving at the age of fifteen, he joined Yorkshire Engine Company as a junior clerk, and later did National Service with the Royal Engineers in Nairobi, Kenya. Following a brief time with Easterbrook & Allcard, Hadfields and Firth Brown Tools, he joined Markham & Co in 1961, remaining there until his retirement in 1997. An early interest in railways broadened to include industrial archaeology, for which Sheffield provided an ideal location. Interest in Markham's past was encouraged by Managing Director, W H Taylor, who made him company historian, and together they ensured that vital archive material relating to the firm was saved, work Peter continued after Mr Taylor retired. On closure of the company, he arranged for the removal of historical material to a place of safe-keeping, and most of it now resides with the Derbyshire Record Office in Matlock.

12. CELEBRATED CONFECTIONS AND MONSTER CAKES

Brian Austin was born in Derby in 1934, but in 1945 transferred to Chesterfield, where he was a pupil at the Grammar School. He claims that his youth was spent in local pubs and dance halls, over snooker tables, and on football and cricket pitches. In 1952 he moved on to study at Nottingham University, and saw National Service in Malaya (now Malaysia) with the 11th Hussars. Brian qualified as a shoemaker and management lecturer, and was elected a Fellow of the British Boot and Shoe Institution. He has worked in developing countries with ILO and BESO, and spent a year in Chesterfield's twin town of Yangquan in Northern China. Since 1980, Brian has been researching Chesterfield's social history, and his ambition is to read every pre-1830 issue of the *Derby Mercury*, which is held on microfilm in Chesterfield Local Studies Library. Part of his field research has involved him in work on a market stall, and he frequently photographs Chesterfield people and places.

INDEX